DATE DUE		
JUL 1 5 1982 NOV 8 1985		
JUL 2 4 1982 JAN 2 6 1984		
SEP 7 1982 MAY 2 8 1986		
SEP 2 1 1982 MAY 2 4 1985		
OCT 9 1982 JUL 11 1988		
JAN 2 2 1983		
MAR 8 1983		
MAR 2 3 1983		
MAY 0 5 1983		
AUG 2 0 1985		
SEP 6 1985		

Teague, Ellen Crawford

I conquered my mountain

I
conquered
my mountain

I

conquered my mountain

the autobiography of Ellen Crawford Teague

PHOENIX PUBLISHING

Canaan, New Hampshire

Teague, Ellen C.
  I conquered my mountain.

  1. Teague, Ellen C. 2. Businessmen—New Hamp-
shire—Biography. 3. Mount Washington Railway. I.
Title.
HE2754.T4A35   385'.6'0924   [B]   82-631
ISBN 0-914016-84-9   AACR2

Printed in the United States of America
by Courier Printing Company
Binding by New Hampshire Bindery
Design by A. L. Morris

To "Art"

Contents

Preface

THESE MEMOIRS are of my own times and include thirty-three years of working at the Cog Railway. They were enjoyable and I wish to share them with others. Therefore I am willing to risk writing this portrait of myself for I am proud to know that I have contributed in a small way to the history and progress of American transportation.

My late husband and I worked side by side in the development, expansion, and improvement of the Mount Washington Cog Railway. After Art's death it took determination to continue the course he charted so well.

More than my memoirs are recounted here. The central character in this story is the Cog Railway, the supporting cast are members of the Teague family and our faithful employees, all of whom felt so privileged to be associated with America's most unusual railroad.

My many friends and associates in the North Country urged and inspired me to write this book and I trust that what I have said will prove worthy of being read. Above all, I hope that I have been able to convey something of the deep affection and admiration I had for my husband, Arthur S. Teague. Without his love, vision, and strength this story would never have been possible.

Ellen Crawford Teague

Philadelphia, Pennsylvania
January 15, 1982

*I
conquered
my mountain*

The Summit, circa 1950.

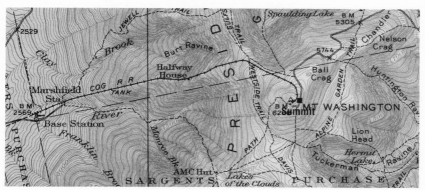

HE CONDUCTOR *glanced at his watch, drew a deep breath, and in true railroad tradition cried:* "All aboard!"
The century-old command echoed down the wooden plat-form, now coated with snow and ice, where a group of men and women was standing, reluctant to leave the breathtaking view from the summit of Mount Washington on this October twelfth afternoon.

"All aboard for the Sunset Special—last train to the Base Station!" He was a bit more insistent this time, and the crowd began to move slowly toward the yellow passenger coach which rested against the **Great Gulf,** *one of the Mount Washington Cog Railway's seven engines with their slanting boilers. As the last passenger entered the car the conductor glanced about the platform, vacant now except for an attractive older woman.*

"Ready, Mrs. Teague?"

1

She nodded, then climbed the frosted steps as he signaled to the engineer.

There was a slight hiss of steam, and the coach shuddered and eased forward as the locomotive gradually inched ahead, its large cogwheel turning slowly and securely engaging each of the cogs on the rack between the tracks. Scheduled train number 6 was on its way—a journey like thousands of others descending the mountain, the powerful little engine leading the way as it held the passenger coach from hurtling down the steep incline.

Number 6 was no ordinary trip today. True, this was the last timetable run of the 1981 season, but more significantly, it marked the end of a era for both the railroad and its owner, Ellen Crawford Teague. October 12, 1981, was memorable because it was Ellen's last ride on a scheduled run as owner and president of the railroad. For the past half-century it had been lovingly and painstakingly operated by Teagues—first Henry, then Arthur, and finally Ellen. Hereafter the running of the world's first mountain-climbing cog railway would be entrusted to others.

Now as the sun began to set far to the west over Vermont's Green Mountains, the nearby slopes were turned to burnished gold. It was a scene Ellen Teague had enjoyed many times but never under circumstances such as she was experiencing this moment. A flood of memories flashed through her mind. Predominating were sharp images of Art, his love and his smile, and of their beloved railroad. Her children came into view too, especially Fanny, Janie, and Charles, who had been as devoted to the road as she. This vision gave way to a blur of faces which she recognized as the men and women who had been so loyal and helpful all those years.

There was a slight lurch to the left, and Ellen knew the train had reached the top of the steep grade. From now on the engine would seem to be working just as hard to hold the car back as it had to push it on the uphill trip. Looking down the aisle, she stared at the engine, and as she did the view gradually diffused, then came into focus again—this time in her imagination she saw the upright boiler of that granddad of them all—Old Peppersass. Yes, Old Peppersass, the first engine Sylvester Marsh had built to start his operation way back in 1869, Sylvester Marsh, without whom there would never have been the Cog Railway . . .

1

World's First Cog Railway

JOURNEY WITH ME back to 1869 on a Saturday, July 3, when Assistant Superintendent Rowell telegraphed that the Mount Washington railway was completed and that trains were running to the Tip-Top House. We are told this was the greatest triumph of railway engineering up to that time in the United States. Sylvester Marsh, a son of New Hampshire, aided by the skill of other New Hampshiremen, had created the first cog railway built to the summit of any mountain in the world!

This undertaking took great vision and enterprise. It was constructed on three and a half miles of trestle and took three years to build. The cost of building the roadbed and the cost of the rolling stock at that time reached $150,000, and every bit of lumber which was used in the railway construction was cut at the steam sawmill at the base depot. The total amount of lumber used in the railbed was 800,000 feet.

Mount Washington is in the heart of the White Mountains, and its summit is 6,293 feet above sea level. It is the highest peak north of the Carolinas and east of the Mississippi River. No one knows which of the early explorers saw it first from the ocean, but the first white man to climb it was Darby Field, who made his ascent in 1642. Mount Washington not only is the highest peak but the most famous, and it is conveniently reached by the Cog Railway.

The only way, a century ago, for Marsh to get into the base of Mount Washington was over a crude road extending six miles from a

The Marshfield Base under construction in 1870.

point at what is now Fabyans Station on Route 302. It used to be the tollgate and was formerly called the Giant's Grave, which was a large mound of river ground deposited by the Ammonoosuc River. Our present Base Road today, which was Marsh's crude road, is the original Crawford Path that was marked and cut in 1821 by Ethan Allen Crawford for whose father, Abel Crawford, Crawford Notch was named. This was the new trail up Mount Washington. Later, in 1841, Crawford cut a path from the base to the summit over which later the Cog Railway was built. The roadbed was laid out by Colonel Freeman of Lancaster, New Hampshire, the son-in-law of Ethan Allen Crawford. In 1853, after Marsh patented his "rack-and-pinion" design for a cog railway as well as an "atmospheric" brake, he applied to the New Hampshire legislature asking for a charter to build a railway up Mount Washington. His model caused great merriment among the legislators; one legislator suggested that while the lawmakers were at it, they should give Marsh permission to extend his track to the moon. The bill passed, however, and Governor William Haile signed it on June 25, 1858.

Marsh's plans for the roadbed started from a point 2,668 feet above the level of the sea and 3,265 feet below the summit. The average grade was 25 percent or 1,300 feet to the mile and the maximum grade over Jacob's Ladder 37.41 percent or 1,980 feet to the mile. Actual construction did not get under way until a year after the Civil War, and in May 1866 Marsh began building the railway track.

At this point, I should tell you what the cog track looks like. If you have seen or ridden on the Cog Railway recently, perhaps it would amaze you to know that the basic features of the railway today are the same as they were in 1869. The track is 56.75-inch gauge and between the rails is a cograil. This cograil is formed by two parallel angle irons, 4 inches apart and connected by 1.5-inch-diameter spools or round steel bars which act as cogs. It looks like a ladder or rack but is known as the cograil. Traction is by the cogwheel engaging cogs which form a rack or cograil between the tracks. The locomotive wheels are not used for traction or braking. The wheels are free on their axles, and no other steam railroad in the world is built with such steep gradients. The steepness is so great most of the way that it is necessary to use locomotives with slanting boilers to maintain operating efficiency. The car seats also slant.

Sylvester Marsh's first locomotive is a museum piece and is now on display at the base of Mount Washington. It was originally called *Hero*

The "George Stephenson" and an open coach at the Summit in the early 1870s.

later nicknamed *Old Peppersass* because of its resemblance to a cruet. It was built by Campbell, Whittier & Company, of Roxbury, Massachusetts, under the supervision of Marsh's son, John F., a civil engineer.

When descending, *Old Peppersass* or any of our other locomotives did not have to use the mechanical brake, as is still true today. Instead, the steam to the cylinders is shut off and air lines to the cylinders are opened. The steam cylinders thus become air compressors when the coach pushes the locomotive downgrade. As in our present locomotives, the flow of air to cylinders can be controlled to obtain different braking pressures. The hand brakes were used only for an emergency, as they are now. *Old Peppersass* and several other vertical boilers, such as the *George Stephenson,* built by Walter Aiken who was Marsh's right-hand man in his enterprise, were discarded in the 1880s when one-hundred-horsepower, eighteen-ton, slanting-boiler (horizontal-boiler) locomotives with four cylinders were placed in service.

On August 29, 1866, *Old Peppersass* made her first test pushing a flatcar with forty passengers up an incline of 15 degrees. By demonstrating its practicability, Marsh financed the company, but had to pay a great deal out of his own pocket. In 1867 Marsh extended the tract to Waumbek, a distance of a little over one mile. During the

OLD PEPPERSASS had a vertical freely suspended woodburning boiler so that its firebox would remain level during its trips. It weighed about four tons and was rated at twenty-five horsepower. This locomotive employed traction and braking which are still used, and it cost the modest little sum of $3,000 to build. The two steam-cylinder piston rods of *Old Peppersass* extended to a transverse crank shaft. This shaft was fitted with a brake drum and drive pinion. The pinion drove a spur gear mounted on a cogwheel shaft so that a gear reduction of about 5 to 1 was obtained. Also on the drive shaft was a ratchet wheel. The ratchet wheel could be held fast by a hand-controlled pawl. In ascending, the cogwheel teeth engaged with the cograil and the locomotive pushed a coach. The coach also was fitted with a pawl and ratchet, and a hand brake acting on a drum mounted on the drive-pinion shaft.

"Old Peppersass" on display at the Marshfield Station.

following May 1868 work was resumed and in eighty-four days the track advanced over one mile and was extended to the top of Jacob's Ladder. This is the steepest of all grades and an exciting part of the trip to the summit, as the train goes on a trestle of 37.41 percent incline. In the fall of 1868 the track was completed within three quarters of a mile from the summit. Work had to be stopped by October 16 because of the severe cold and snow that set in, but Marsh still had five-hundred feet remaining to reach the true geographical summit. The following June work was again resumed, and in three weeks' time, on July 3, the track was completed and trains ran for the first time from the base of Mount Washington to Tip-Top House, the true geographical summit. In 1870 more than five-thousand persons were carried by the Cog Railway.

Walter Aiken became Marsh's manager and was the largest individual stockholder. Walter was the son of Herrick Aiken of Franklin, New Hampshire, who had previously conceived the idea of ascending Mount Washington by cog. Herrick had made two ascents on horseback and had built a model of the roadbed and track with cog and engine. Prominent men had discouraged Herrick, but Sylvester Marsh had studied Herrick's model in 1852.

Nine former patents between 1829 and 1839 were helpful to Marsh and Aiken, but the two most important were a patent issued to William Bent of Philadelphia, Pennsylvania, in 1832, for cogwheels for propelling railway cars up inclines, and Nathan Reed's of Belfast, Maine, in 1836, for improvements on railways. This last model was exhibited in the Rotunda in the Capitol in Washington, D.C.

Walter Aiken was a very remarkable man, and it is to him we should give a great deal of credit, since under his guidance the railway became a financial success and remained so as long as he lived. He died in 1893. Walter Aiken was a machinist and an inventor; he was practical and energetic, and his judgment was sound. He was responsible for perfecting Marsh's inventions and adapting them to practical use in the railway. Walter never spared himself when work had to be done.

The fame of the Mount Washington Cog Railway soon spread far and wide. The railroads from east and west (the present Maine Central and Boston & Maine) reached Fabyans in 1874 and 1875, and in 1876 a branch was built to the base to connect with the Cog Railway.

The Boston & Maine Railroad took over the Cog Railway in 1883, but it was not until 1931 that the B. & M. sold out to Colonel Henry Nelson Teague. "The Colonel," as he was called, was a longtime friend of Edward S. French, president of the Boston & Maine and a very dear friend of his assistant, Lawrence F. Whitmore.

Henry Teague was born on Mount Desert Island, Maine, on June 2, 1875, and graduated from Dartmouth College in 1900. He was the first graduate from its Amos Tuck School of Finance in 1901. Henry Teague was no ordinary individual. He was quite a tall person, approximately six feet three inches, and weighed about 250 pounds. When Henry spoke, his voice bellowed, so that he attracted attention. When he failed to command the attention he wanted, he would become cross and hammer his old silver-tipped brown cane.

Henry was a great promoter and driver with his business. He would visit every convention throughout the White Mountains and stop at every hotel he could think of to leave his brochure. Business was stimulated because of his continuous supervision, and the railroad prospered as its reputation spread and an increasing number of tourists came for the unique mountain ride.

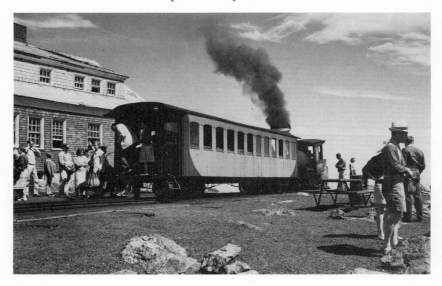

Coach No. 2 at the Summit.

I had never visited Mount Washington or the railroad before I met Uncle Henry Teague, as he came to be known, but now I am getting ahead of my story and so must go back to the beginning.

"The Great Gulf" descending Mt. Washington near the marker.

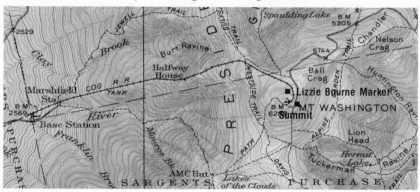

*L*IKE THE PULLMAN CONDUCTOR who can judge train speed, position, and performance by the clackity-clack rhythm of the heavy steel wheels as they pass over the rail joints, Ellen Teague's countless rides on her Cog Railway with its unique ratchety sound gave her a sixth sense which told her whether or not all was well. This afternoon the engine was performing perfectly, and now the little train had just gone over the summit line and was on the steep incline.

A moment later Ellen saw the weathered sign by the track commemorating the death of Lizzie Bourne who froze to death at this very spot in 1855–just a few hundred feet from the summit and safety. Lizzie Bourne, Ellen reflected, was one of the many unlucky ones who had misjudged the mountain's wrath and pushed ahead in raging blizzards, only to lose the gamble. Glancing away from Lizzie's marker, Ellen looked off to the right in

11

time to see a group of hikers nearing the summit, evidently planning to stay overnight.

She could not help but admire the spirit and determination of those who eschewed riding her railroad because they wanted to experience the exhilaration and satisfaction which come from actually climbing, but how much easier it would have been to have come up by train! Still, the train had not always been there either, and how many of those who had trudged up the mountain over the past century and a half knew that her distant relatives, that "giant of a man" Abel Crawford and his son, Ethan Allen, had cut the first path from the notch up to the summit in 1819? Since then thousands of men, women, and children have owed those two a debt of gratitude!

Thinking about the Crawfords—and of her own name, for she was a Crawford before her marriage—Ellen felt an understandable sense of pride in her heritage. She was especially proud of the fact that she had carried on the tradition established by Henry and Arthur Teague to keep the railway running no matter what the cost. Over the years it had become increasingly important to the state's economy, attracting thousands of tourists each year. Furthermore, without the chugging engines and dedicated employees, those who were unable or unwilling to hike would never have been able to reach Mount Washington's famed summit.

Yes, on the whole it had been a good life, but her hardships were nothing compared with those of the earlier Crawfords and other pioneers who explored the mountains, cut roads, opened inns for travelers, and made it possible for all to enjoy the spectacular mountain views.

"Memories—yes," Ellen murmured to herself, "this is a day for memories, indeed." And, as the train continued its jog down the mountain, she wondered whether or not she too had proved worthy of those other courageous and hardworking Crawfords.

2

Childhood Years

MY FATHER was born on July 17, 1869, just two weeks after the Cog Railway started operating! He was the youngest son of Dr. David McLean Crawford who practiced medicine in Mifflintown, Juniata County, Pennsylania, in 1864. His forebears for four generations were Scottish doctors. I trace my father's ancestors back to the reign of Mary Queen of Scots when the Crawfords were followers of John Knox and fled from Ayrshire, Scotland, to northern Ireland and settled in Counties Tyrone, Derry, Colrain, and Donegal.

A year after George Washington was inaugurated as our first president, my great-great-grandfather, James Crawford, sailed from northern Ireland with his family and half brother, Thomas, to join other Crawfords who had arrived earlier, some of them having fought in the American Revolutionary War.

Another branch of the family (to which I am not directly related) migrated from Scotland to County Tyrone, Ireland, and John Crawford was born there around 1675, emigrating to Connecticut in 1733. Some of these Crawfords eventually moved on to Guildhall, Vermont, which is just north of Lancaster, New Hampshire, where they married members of the Rosebrook family who had already settled there.

In 1791 Abel Crawford moved from Guildhall to Giant's Grave near Bretton Woods, New Hampshire, and shortly thereafter relocated farther south in Northland, also known as Hart's Location, at the lower end of what is now known as Crawford Notch. His famous son, Ethan Allen, was born in 1792, and both father and son became legendary figures in the history of this region. Readers interested in

13

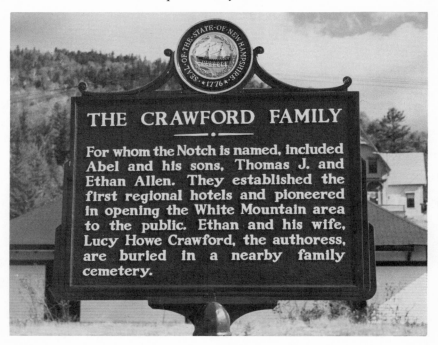

The marker at Fabyan Station.

learning more about them will enjoy *Lucy Crawford's History of the White Mountains*. Lucy was Ethan Allen's wife and first published this story in 1846, the year her husband died.

A distant cousin of mine, Fred Crawford, a direct descendant of Abel and Ethan Allen, now owns the Old Home Crawford, in Guildhall, Vermont. I owned the farmhouse and lot numbers 5 and 6 which once belonged to the Rosebrooks and Abel Crawford in the same town. The fifth owner, I sold the farm in 1973.

The famous Crawford House which once stood at the head of Crawford Notch is now only a memory, but the Crawford name will be perpetuated forever in the beautiful notch which bears the name.

Introducing Ellen Crawford

I am a woman of mild disposition, in command of my temper, cheerfully good-humored, and capable of sentiment. It took me thirty-three years to "conquer my mountain" and realize the satisfaction which comes from devoting most of one's energies to assuring the continuation of a public trust. This was how I conceived my responsibility, just as Art, my husband, did up to the time of his death. I have suffered wear and tear of body and mind from incredible problems and emotional crises, and sometimes I wonder how I ever was able to conquer my mountain.

I have found as I write of my experiences at the Mount Washington Cog Railway that each step of my life seems to have fit together naturally, just as the many parts of a puzzle fall into place. I certainly never thought that each incident in my life would prepare me for my railway experience, and it must be due to my Scottish durability that I have been able to cope with my responsibilities at the Cog Railway.

The White Mountains of New Hampshire which I call home are beautiful beyond compare. They are part of me now, and so are "my people" of the North Country, all those wonderful men and women who have befriended me in one way or another and whose lives touched mine. Before telling you about my thirty-three years at the Cog Railway, however, I would like to share with you a bit of my early life.

Family Background

Mother, who was Frances Josephine Stratton before her marriage, was born in Germantown, Pennsylvania, in 1877. Although only five feet two inches tall, her independent and demanding personality made up for her short stature, and she was greatly admired. Father, Dr. Edgar Druitt Crawford, was born in 1869 in Mifflintown, Pennsylvania. A tall good-looking man, he was always calm, gracious, and generous. He loved his family deeply; he was compassionate in his practice, and all his patients adored him.

My earliest recollection of him goes back to the year 1917 when I was four years old. I remember hearing my father calling to my mother, "War has been declared," which left a deep impression on me. Subsequently each of us was given one small glass of sugar, which was placed on the dining room table and was to last for a month. I also can recall the large barrel of flour on the sharp curving back stairs which led to my bedroom above the kitchen. Our kitchen had a large coal stove with a hot-water heater by its side and a big coal scuttle between the tank and the stove.

I had two sisters, Frances Jane, fifteen months older, and Margaret Murray, thirteen months younger than I. We lived in Penllyn, Montgomery County, Pennsylvania, where our home had been built sometime in the late 1700s and once served as the old parsonage for Boehm's Dutch Reformed Church, whose land adjoined ours.

Our house, a three-story stone-and-stucco structure, was situated between Blue Bell and Penllyn on the Penllyn Pike, overlooking Gwynedd Valley. What a beautiful view it was with its five acres of gardens and lush fields where we ran and played as children!

Mother and Father raised all their vegetables. During World War I, Mother and our Irish maid, Rose Anne Flynn, canned a thousand jars of produce for home consumption and another thousand jars for the Red Cross to send overseas to help feed our troops.

Some Early Recollections

I can still see the horse-drawn vans of the gypsies who passed our home many times in their caravans. When I was very young, I was so frightened whenever these strange people appeared that I ran inside the house and hid under a table or sofa because we has been warned that "the gypsies would take us away."

Marnie, my younger sister, and I used to hide when we heard the ragman who came with his horse and buggy. He would call, "Rags, rags, any rags to sell?" Our maid occasionally asked him to stop, and we would watch him weigh the number of pounds of cloth. I have no idea what Rose received from him in pennies—it is all just "a memory."

My early winter remembrances were of heavy snows covering the fences between the fields and of the hum of the telephone wires. During cold weather I would push my ear against the telephone pole and listen to a humming sound which I could almost imagine to be voices.

I remember we had two horses and a pony named Dot who had previously been in Barnum & Bailey's Circus. The markings of the Welsh pony were brown dots with an all-white base and a huge brown saddlelike patch across his back. Father would take us riding in the sleigh, and sometimes we would attach our sleds to the back of it. We had loads and loads of healthy country fun, especially when Marnie and I would build caves in the snowdrifts.

Marnie and I were usually into something. I remember one particular evening when Mother and Father were entertaining a few guests, we went upstairs to our rooms where we took off our clothes and painted our bodies to make us look like Indians. After doing this we went down the gracious front staircase and walked into the living room where the adults were talking. I still remember the surprised looks on their faces. Then Father slowly rose from his chair, undid his black leather belt, and started pulling it from his waist. Marnie and I disappeared so quickly he had no chance to use it, but we never forgot that moment.

Summers, especially the July months, I remember well. In the evenings Mother and Father would sit in the gray hammock and slowly swing, barely moving. Father would smoke one cigarette, which he always said was to keep the mosquitoes away. I loved to watch the fireflies, and there were plenty of them in the fields. Often I would catch them in a glass jar and take them up to the sleeping porch where we three girls slept during the hot weather. Eight o'clock was our bedtime, summer and winter.

Our parents sent us to private schools and always to church as well as to Sunday school on Sundays. Mother took us to the Episcopal Saint Thomas Church in Whitemarsh, where the Reverend Nathaniel B. Groton was rector. Mother taught the adult Bible class. She was an Episcopalian, Father a Presbyterian. He never allowed mother to sew on Sundays, nor could we children swim or play cards on the Sabbath.

When I was just fourteen I began attending summer religious conferences of the Episcopal church, run by Father Huntington. I enjoyed his classes and taking notes. One day I asked Father Huntington why my father would not permit us to swim on Sundays. His reply was, "The Lord never said how large the bathtub was." I repeated that answer to my father, and after that we girls had no problems about swimming on the Lord's Day. Father was strict. He believed in tradition, and tradition was not to be broken.

Disobedience and the Devil

I was taught that disobedience was a sin. "Every tree that bringeth not forth good fruit should be hewn down and cast into the fire." Let me go back seven years and recall with pain one incident of disobedience.

It was summer and Mother had taken my sister Jane to the city where Jane had x-ray treatments on her thymus gland. Marnie and I were left at home, as usual with Rose Anne Flynn. Often when we had finished our chores such as dusting, washing out the bathtub, and helping make our beds we were rewarded with a piece of white bread spread with delicious sweet butter and covered with brown sugar. We enjoyed this, but today I craved a real treat—round white peppermints, which I loved.

"Suppose I get five cents from Mother's top bureau drawer," I proposed to Marnie, "then we could get some mints." She nodded enthusiastically. Two minutes later we were sneaking away from Rose and then walked about a mile to the country store at Blue Bell. It was owned by old Mr. Deprefontaine and his son.

In those days I wore bloomers, so after buying the five-for-a-penny mints and spending the five pennies, I tucked the bag of peppermints in my bloomers. We then started home, hoping to return before Rose missed us, but I heard her calling as we approached the house. Well, we were sent to our rooms to sit on our straight chairs, but there were no spanks, at least not until Mother returned. She lost no time using the hairbrush on our proper places, which made it most difficult to sit at dinner that evening.

It was the custom in our home for Mother to come to each of our rooms every night to hear our individual prayers and read the Bible to us. We were always taught to ask forgiveness of our sins. One time I asked God to "Please kill the devil so I can have peace the rest of my life." Mother told me sometime later that, on hearing about this particular prayer, Father laughed himself to sleep.

I was a very active child and was always up to something. When our dogs died, I would bury them. Once, after several years passed, I dug one up and tried to wire the bones together. I guess I came by my medical instincts naturally, for people used to say, "Ellen will end up being a doctor." I often helped the cats deliver their kittens in the barn, becoming quite upset if the mother cat ate her first batch. It was normal for me to examine the kittens and try to determine which were male and which female.

School Days

Miss Hensey's school in Ambler provided my first experience in private school. I started kindergarten there and attended for two years. My sister Jane and I had a piano teacher, Miss Dorothy, who taught us to play a duet which we performed at the end of the school year. To reach my second private school, Miss Wilson's on Pine Street in Philadelphia, I had to take the train from Penllyn to the Reading terminal. It was not dangerous because in those days the conductors supervised the schoolchildren and saw to it that they behaved. We were taught to be courteous to our elders. I enjoyed running down all those many, many steps at the Reading terminal to catch the number 18 trolley in the morning on my way to school. The conductor on "the 3:02 train" after school was good to the children and always greeted us with, "How be ye?" We soon started calling him "How be ye."

Private schools were taught by members of old Philadelphia families in those days. I remember the handshake each morning and quietly taking our seats to learn; the beginning of French lessons; the continuing of my piano lessons; and the hot dogs, beans, and tomato soup for lunch in school. There was no talking or rushing in the halls and always a quiet dismissal at the end of the school day.

My third private school experience was at the Wharton School, run by Miss Rosa and Miss Nellie Wharton, members of one of Philadelphia's oldest families. They were severe and strict teachers. While attending Wharton several of my school friends were invited to spend the weekend with us at Penllyn. That was when I had "the very bad accident" with my foot.

"The Very Bad Accident"

Marnie and I had decided not to harness the pony Dot but give our friends a ride in the pony cart with Marnie pulling between the shafts and me pushing the cart out the driveway and up the Penllyn Pike.

After going a distance Marnie tried to turn the cart around, but it was too heavy for her and it started rolling back toward me and the embankment. I quickly jumped up on the embankment so the cart's sharp steel step would not go through my stomach, but the step caught my right foot, which was in a sneaker, and severed the bones, leaving my foot hanging.

It was quite awhile before I could get x-rayed and taken down to Jefferson Hospital. I remember Dr. Thomas Shallow talking to me and my begging him not to cut my leg off. Tetanus set in and I became a very sick girl. I stayed in the hospital almost six weeks and then was in a cast for a long time. God was good to me, and Dr. Shallow was too; he was able to scrape all the bones, and had to put drains in my foot for many weeks.

The author at seven.

I still have no feeling in four of the toes on my right foot. I recovered with much experience behind me and, at eight years of age, decided that when I grew up I would be a nurse.

Agnes Irwin School

I entered sixth grade in the Agnes Irwin School, then located at 2009-2011 Delancey Place. Mother taught the Bible there for twenty-five years. She had obtained her Bible credits by taking examinations with learned scholars and was accredited through what was then known as the National Council in New York.

The Agnes Irwin School offers many advantages for girls and is now located in Rosemont, on the main line outside Philadelphia. Miss Josephine A. Natt was headmistress when I went to school and taught me Latin for four years. I hated Latin translations, so I used a pony, but it was easy to memorize the vocabulary and learn the grammar.

My senior year at school was crammed with studies, examinations, and social events. I enjoyed school, especially my English and poetry classes. Miss Lent, a University of Rochester graduate, taught my English classes and was an excellent teacher. My old friend, Nellie Graff, was another beloved teacher. Tall, thin, and with gray hair, she never raised her voice above a whisper. She encouraged me in my writing, and she said that I had a natural talent. She wrote several books about Maine, and after graduation I continued to keep in touch with her for some time. She died several years ago.

I have many fond memories of my years at Agnes Irwin. They were formative, growing years, complete with good friends, good teachers, a wholesome atmosphere, and much encouragement to make something of my life.

During my freshman year I had been asked to be treasurer of our athletic association; I accepted and it was fun. We Crawford girls were good athletes, and I usually made the first teams.

My Social Life

I think I attended dancing school throughout my entire young life. At first it consisted of Thursday afternoon classes, then the Friday evening, and finally the Saturday evening classes. Our hostess was Mrs. Audaine Duer, granddaughter of Edgar Allan Poe.

I am grateful for my early education and the good times too. I was a member of the dramatic club, the music club, and the art club—we were allowed to join only three organizations. My school years also were filled with social activities, including dances, teas, and football games. Since I had several first cousins at Annapolis and West Point, I spent many weekends away. Clarence Rodgers, who came from Wyoming, was one of my first beaus and was on the polo team at West Point. I went with Clarence for a year and a half to dances and football games at the Point. He became a Rhodes scholar.

During my school years I saw many of the Army-Navy games and on Thanksgiving Day shivered through the Penn-Cornell game. Mother and Father were members of the Penllyn Club where on Sundays they had polo games and paper chases on horseback. In summer, after playing tennis and swimming, we dressed up and attended the fashionable teas served by club members.

In my high school years the boys whom I considered good friends spent many weekends at our home in Penllyn, mainly because most dances were held on Saturday nights and Father would not let the boys bring us home. We were annoyed at first but eventually accepted his judgment. I invited the boys, and Father was always there waiting for us after the dances to drive us home with our dates. I must say we had great times in those days, as did our friends, a few of whom I shall mention here.

First, there was Bill Creighton who was attending the University of Pennsylvania and loved to tango. Later he became Episcopal bishop of Washington, D.C., at the Cathedral of Saints Peter and Paul. He retired several years ago.

Then there was Dick Bull whose father was an old beau of Mother's. Dick studied law at the University of Pennsylvania and later married a cousin of mine, Josephine Rothermel. Dick became an associate of the law firm of Raybourn & White. The Whites once lived in the house below us in Penllyn.

Nor should I forget Dick Curtis of the Curtis Publishing Company and Curtis Flying Field. Dick was lots of fun to be with, especially when our crowd went to a dance.

Finally I want to say something about Walter Reichardt who was, and still is, my closest friend from those school years. He too attended the University of Pennsylvania and won the Grand Prix de Rome in 1929. He loved our countryside and often came out to be with us so that he could enjoy the country, paint, and take me to dances. Walter has always kept close contact throughout these many years. He lives in California, and several years ago when I was attending a convention in Vancouver, British Columbia, I flew down to Los Angeles for an exciting weekend reunion with Walter and his family, whom I had known for some time.

I have always been eager to be successful. I have wanted to work and get ahead. I am persistent. I have tried to the best of my ability to apply the talents which God has bestowed upon me. I enjoy people and most of all I like to help those who are less fortunate and have not had my advantages. I feel my early religious background gave me insight and proved helpful in my nursing career as well as in all my relations with people.

I have had the privilege of talking with many prominent and wise men of the church. Some of these scholars included Father Huntington of the order of the Holy Cross; Bishop Overs of Liberia; and Dr. Suter of the Episcopal church, who has written many books on theology.

All this has given me a sense of security and self-confidence. Following graduation from the Agnes Irwin School in 1931 and the excitement of debutante parties, white gowns, and flowers, I was ready to taste knowledge on my own at whatever cost.

Engine No. 2, The "George Stephenson," built in 1869.

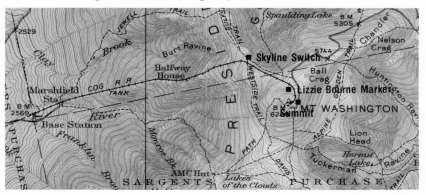

*T*HE TRAIN'S SPEED *gradually slackened, and the Cog's slower rhythm joined Ellen's thoughts from her early childhood to the train. Evidently the engineer was going to stop at Skyline siding, although the timetable did not call for a scheduled halt there. A prudent move, Ellen thought, for no doubt in the gathering twilight he wanted to make certain that the switches were set correctly. No point taking a chance on this, the last trip of the season!*

She was correct. The fireman was climbing down to the track and a moment later returned, got aboard, and the train started up. It clattered over the switch points and then settled into its familiar clanking sound. The switch incident brought up another memory—after all, this was a day for memories, wasn't it? Yes, and now it was Art's turn because he and Lawrence Richardson had worked together on what are known as the most complicated switches in the world.

25

These devices may be intricate, but they can easily be worked by one man; in fact, it takes less than five minutes for the shiftover and passing of locomotives. To throw a switch, the brakeman lifts seven separate pieces of rail and moves two levers. This is done so that the ascending train can pull over on the side track to allow the descending train to continue on through to the Base Station.

There are a total of three switches: one at the Base Station for the convenience of switching trains; one at Waumbek stop, which is one third of the way; and Skyline switch, two thirds of the way up. It is near this Skyline switch that the famed Appalachian Trail, which extends from Maine to Georgia, crosses under the Mount Washington Cog Railway tracks.

The railway had just one track before the early 1930s, and with the installation of these three switches traffic increased rapidly. Trains were now able to run on the hour and every hour from the base to the summit from July through Labor Day. Once the switches had been installed and multiple train operation was possible, passenger traffic quickly jumped more than three fold.

Reflecting on the switches, Ellen smiled, thinking of Tower A under Manhattan's Park Avenue where five men stand before a schematic diagram of the Conrail tracks over which hundreds of trains make their way daily into and out of Grand Central Station. How different from her railway! The Cog switches were complicated enough, she knew, but nothing compared with the tortuous switch patterns often required in the Park Avenue tunnel. To work those switches, however, a man has only to pull or push a lever or two and the work is done electrically for him. Furthermore, a set of interlocking relays and other gadgets prevents errors—a far cry from switching on her little road! She closed her eyes as she remembered the terrible accident of 1967 when someone either tampered with or failed to set the switch correctly and the railway suffered its first and only passenger fatalities.

That, however, was but one of the many crises she had experienced over her lifetime, just one of the tragedies which were marked by suffering and pain and called for expert medical care, which was given by Dr. Harry McDade and others. Odd how often she had become involved in accidents—able to use her medical knowledge and draw on her early training as a nurse. Of course, nursing school—how many years ago, how young she was—and how much she subsequently appreciated the value of that training throughout her whole life! Nursing school . . . Thomas Jefferson University Hospital . .

26

3

My Nursing Experience

WHEN I GRADUATED from high school, I knew I wanted to study nursing and at a good accredited hospital. I visited Women's Medical College, Johns Hopkins University, and Thomas Jefferson University and decided on the latter because I liked its certification best. I sent in my application and was informed that my knowledge of chemistry was inadequate.

Father called a staff member, Dr. Pascal Brooke Bland, the internationally famous doctor in obstetrics. After he agreed to sponsor and vouch for me, I was notified that I should take several tests. I then was accepted and entered Thomas Jefferson University on February 4, 1932.

I knew this would be my life for at least three solid years with no play or foolishness, all study and dedication. I knew nothing would stop me, since now I had the opportunity to take up new studies and a profession worth working for.

Training to Be a Nurse

There were thirty-two girls in my class and my room was in the old nurses home at 1020 Spruce Street, Philadelphia, on the third floor front. It was small but I found that the atmosphere and excitement of the place soon made me forget its size. Getting started on my studies was exciting. They included organic and inorganic chemistry, laboratory work, materia medica, surgical nursing, operating room technique, ethics, bacteriology, public health, principals and practice of nursing, bandaging, method of massage—and lectures, lectures,

27

lectures. There were so many wonderful things to learn and I could actually feel myself growing inside. I cannot describe this sensation except to say it was almost a hurt feeling, expanding within. I knew I had chosen the right work because I was happy, even though it was a twelve-hour work-and-study routine.

I had to be in by nine at night and up at six in the morning, washed, and dressed in my pink uniform with the long sleeves and white cuffs and starched white apron. My hair was pinned back so that I looked neat and orderly. Student nurses had to sign in at the hospital each morning for breakfast at six-thirty. We had two free hours each day, a half day each week, and a late pass until eleven-thirty once a month. My probationary period lasted four months, and after passing the required exams, I was capped and fully accepted as a student in the hospital.

Ward duty began at ten minutes of seven each morning. Miss Clara Melville, the nursing school head, made her ward rounds each morning and each evening. She was indeed a dedicated woman, a woman who reminded me of Clara Barton. My first ward assignment was in the bronchoscopic department on the men's ward with six patients in one room and four in another. Each white enamel bed had a matching white enamel stand to its right, and on top of the stand were a large sixteen-ounce graduate (glass flask) for expectoration and a pile of unsterilized gauze called clinics. These clinics were put over the patient's mouth when she or he coughed. A paper bag, pinned to the bed to hold the soiled guaze, had to be burned in the incinerator at the end of each day. The odor from the glass graduates, even though covered with a brown bag, was nauseating. One of my first jobs was to empty these and sterilize them with Lysol, using a long-handled brush to clean them properly and thoroughly. I found it hard to make myself do this, but I knew I had to conquer such reactions if I were to succeed as a nurse. I really felt sorry for a young classmate of mine when she emptied her first bedpan. She just could not take it, and when she failed to come out of the bathroom I went in and found the poor girl dreadfully sick. She left training after that.

I soon was taught how to watch patients come out of anesthesia. This was a privilege because I learned how to handle the situation and now had opportunity to accept responsibility. My next assignment was the accident ward where I experienced some of my first exciting duties. I gave tetanus antitoxin shots, assisted with spinal punctures, and took smears and delivered the slides to the lab for cultures. I enjoyed taking blood pressures and meeting patients and found it exciting to see so many types of cases. There were attempted suicides; drunks; syphilitic and gonococcal cases; patients with allergies and with severe burns; beaten, bruised, and cut patients; spinal meningitis suspects; and always the unexpected. It was an eye-opener when I encountered, even back then, the large number of theatrical people who were on drugs and came into the accident ward to get codeine and other drugs from the doctors. Each department was different, and all were intriguing.

I next trained in the gynecological, women's medical, and men's special wards. Although this work was fascinating, my first Christmas away from home was hard. I had been assigned night duty on the men's special ward that Christmas Eve. As I entered the room to receive my report, I saw the huge tree decorated at the far end. Then I glanced at the two rows of sick patients. They included two severely burned cases just brought in after a truck loaded with Christmas toys had turned over, caught fire, and exploded at Sixty-ninth Street. It almost made me sick. Tears came to my eyes and I swallowed hard; it was a difficult night.

When I look back, I realize that being busy and having to think of others was the beginning of my maturing. My patients were dependent on me, and my work had to be done, so that I was quite aware of the need for self-denial. I felt that growth within me, and strange as it may seem, I experienced happiness. The Christmas season passed, and I knew that the hospital was my home and that the patients were my brothers. Somehow God helped me get through that night, and I had become what I had always wanted to be, a colleague with my fellow workers.

Night duty in the women's surgical ward had much to offer. I was responsible for forty patients in the big ward plus a postoperative room across the hall. I gave the patients their medicines, wrote up their reports, watched the intravenous injections, and gave special attention to those who needed it. If I did not have enough time to finish my work, I would call the principal nurse who would relieve me so that I could go for my midnight snack.

My next assignment was in the diet kitchen, which covered the metabolic study of different diets for disorders and diseases such as ulcers, with special U1 and U2 diets, or diabetes, with the weighing and figuring of carbohydrates, proteins, and fats. This was interesting for a while because I had to cook the food for the special diets and

The author in nursing school.

push it to the wards in a large metal cart. The assignment eventually became monotonous but was instructive nevertheless. I was relieved when the required training was completed because I was dreaming about calories in my sleep, repeating over and over that "a calorie is the amount of heat necessary to raise one gram of heat one degree centigrade."

Upon leaving the diet kitchen, I went to the maternity ward, and I loved every moment of my training in this branch of medicine. Here was the indescribable thrill of holding a new life, a baby as it was delivered from its mother, truly golden moments in my life. However, there were many tense moments too when crucial decisions had to be made by the doctors. There were high and low forceps, sections when necessary, and of course mostly normal deliveries. It was a privilege to work with so many courageous physicians and listen to their final decisions, what they felt was best for both mother and child. To know their ups and downs and their concerns, and just to be able to be of assistance to them, brought great satisfaction. What a wonderful reward after working long hours, to receive a sincere thank you!

The Tragic Side of Nursing

Of course, there is as much sadness as joy working in a hospital. I will mention just two cases, first the young black girl who had given birth to her first child. She was a good patient, had no problems with her delivery, and was preparing to go home with her child. While her husband was on his way to the hospital to take her home, the young mother got up from her chair to go to the bathroom. She never made it, and she fell over dead in front of me. This was my first case of this type in which an embolism killed the patient. It was most difficult for me to talk with the father. Strange as it may seem, he opened his arms to his first child and held him close, so close that I could feel the comfort he received from his newborn infant.

The other event I cannot forget occurred when I was on night duty in the men's medical ward, permitting me to experience a glimpse into eternity. I was sitting at the main desk writing my reports after medications had been given and ward rounds made. There was a male nurse on duty with me because we had some very sick patients. I had asked him to double-check some of the patients on the critical list, and not too many minutes had passed when out of the stillness I heard him call, "Miss Crawford, please come here." As I approached the patient's bed, I saw the man raise himself, a beautiful smile lighting

his face. At the same time he stretched out his right arm while he
opened his eyes very wide, almost in astonishment. Then in a won-
drous voice he said, "Oh," and fell back dead. What an unusual
opportunity to have been at his bedside and witness such a happy
ending.

It was never easy for me when I knew a patient's life was coming to
an end. Sometimes they read my thoughts or could see the answer in
my eyes. I have been told often that I speak with my eyes. Perhaps so,
but it makes the answer no easier. I remember a cancer patient who
was so weak toward the end that my heart almost broke. I had been
shaving him each day so he could not look at himself, and one day he
asked me to give him a mirror. I gave it to him. He looked at his
reflection and let out a cry which went through me. Then he said, "I
am dying, it won't be long," and waited for my answer.

I could not respond, and when he saw the tears I was trying to hold
back, he knew my answer. I shared what faith I could with him and
tried to give him peace. When the night nurse came on, I remained on
duty because he asked me to stay on with her. I was very glad I did; he
died that evening.

Inspirational Doctors

I had many friends among the interns and doctors. They relied on
the nurses, and the nurses in turn relied on them when working
together on cases or in the operating room. I found that the doctors
who knew their patients well seemed able to speed their recovery
much better than those who had temporary relationships. I was fortunate in knowing many prominent doctors at Thomas Jefferson. Some
of them included Dr. Frank Braceland, top psychiatrist today in the
Institute of Living in Hartford, Connecticut, now in his late seventies;
and Dr. Joseph Waldman, ophthalmologist, and still a good friend
who used to teach me a new medical word every time we passed each
other in the hospital corridors. I think I became a walking medical
dictionary. Dr. Bruce Nye, Dr. James Surver, and I were known as
"The Three Musketeers." Dr. Nye was the associate dean of Jefferson
Medical College, and his son, Carlyle, who worked quite a few years
at the Mount Washington Cog Railway, is now a cardiologist in
Norfolk, Virginia.

Dr. Warren B. Davis, the internationally known plastic surgeon,
was one of the finest friends I ever had at the hospital. It was a great

privilege to work with him. This genius would rebuild ears by using false cartilage from the ribs; remake faces; and for children born with one eye, he would construct another eye. In other amazing operations he rebuilt noses and harelips and did many skin grafts. He was an unusually kind and generous man.

I should like to record here how much I enjoyed working with Dr. Anspach, Dr. Lyons, Dr. Thomas Shallow, Dr. Reynolds Griffith, Dr. John Montgomery, Dr. Burns, Dr. Mohler, Dr. Bower, Dr. Knowles, and many others.

Pediatrics and private duty on private floors were my remaining assignments before I finished my courses. I then took the hospital examinations which were followed by the state boards, which had to be passed before one was qualified for private duty or general work on the floors. I passed all my examinations in good standing, whereupon I became an active member of the American Red Cross and registered to be on call for active service. At the same time I signed the register in the Thomas Jefferson Hospital and thereafter was assigned to many cases until I resigned in 1942.

Out on My Own

I have lost track of the number of patients I nursed over the next twelve years, but three cases stand out. One of them was destined to change my life and bring me my greatest happiness.

The first case involved a corporation executive, the president of a mining company who, despite his money, was a neglected patient and bedridden with arthritis. He had not been to his Philadelphia office in over a year.

I was called on this case by the Dr. Martin Rehfuss, who developed the Rehfuss tube used for biliary drainage. Dr. Rehfuss discussed the case with me, and then I studied my patient carefully to decide how I should approach him and give him the best of care.

My first observation was that he received no attention from his wife, who spent all her time taking care of her mother. Although there were two Irish maids and a chauffeur, the wife seemed too involved to bother with her husband. Thus, knowing what I had to work with, I began my treatments.

It did not take long to gain this man's confidence. Although I have always been extremely professional in my attitude toward my patients, I have also given them loving-kindness, good care, and the best of medical treatment. He recognized this quickly and recipro-cated with his friendship and cooperation. I knew then that I had a good base for his recovery.

With the doctor's consent I started the effleurage treatment, which is a light massage, on his arms and legs, and very gently but firmly rubbing with an upward movement on his spinal cord. This not only relaxed the patient but slowly stimulated the circulation of his blood. I worked with him twelve hours a day and, after two weeks of applying this massage, noticed that he was no longer grouchy in the morning when I came on duty. I interpreted this as a good sign, so I decided to ask the chauffeur if he would help me put the patient in his bathtub. We soaked him every morning, and at the same time I gave him a special diet, maintaining this treatment for two weeks. Next, the chauffeur and I walked the patient around the house slowly for another week.

After I had been working with this man for almost two months, Dr. Rehfuss said that we might take him out for a ride in his car. As my patient's strength gradually returned, I helped him get to his office and to occasional meetings. All told, I remained with him for ten months. He was a wonderful, dear man, and thinking that he would now be fine, I asked to be relieved from further duty.

After I left I dropped in from time to time to see how he was coming along, but to my dismay his condition seemed to worsen steadily and he died six months later. I had done all I possibly could for him, which is all one can do in the nursing field.

Life Is an Adventure

When I left this case, my father did not want me to take an apart-ment by myself or with a group of nurses, giving me a number of reasons which I accepted. Therefore I took a room at the Deaconess House at Eighth and Spruce streets, Philadelphia, where I met many interesting foreign students, including some fascinating Chinese.

Bishop Taitt's room was next to mine, and we shared the bathroom between us. I very much enjoyed being with this church group. One morning I had just come off a case and was relaxing in the tub when there was a knock on the door.

I called out and Dean Springer answered: "You have just been called to go to Jefferson Hospital on an outside case," she said. I thanked her and quickly dried and dressed while she packed my small suitcase. In those days I had few possessions, so it was easy to tell her where my clothing was and what to pack. Believe it or not, I made it to the hospital in half an hour.

This is how my life has always been since starting my nursing career—it has been an adventure, full of surprises and never dull! When I completed this case and returned to the Deaconess House, Dr. Jeffreys of Christ Church asked me if I would be interested in medical missionary work. He told me that his brother was just returning from China where nurses were needed badly and that the brother would be glad to help me learn the language. Shortly thereafter the National Council of Churches sent someone to interview me, and I had to make my decision soon. Again I felt it best to follow my father's advice. He did not want me to go, and I think that I was not meant for this work inasmuch as he died a year later, and then there was much I had to do to help at home.

My last two cases were involved with one family. I had promised Mother I would be home that first Christmas after Dad died, but that was not meant to be either. Three days before Christmas Dr. Martin Rehfuss called me and asked, as a special favor, if I would take care of a very dear friend of his.

My Most Important Case

After I agreed to take the case, Dr. Rehfuss briefed me on the situation. Major Beckurts, the patient, was a military man who had a urinary tract infection and prostate trouble. He had a wife and daughter but was a lonely man. They lived in one of the best Philadelphia suburbs, were waited on by three servants, and had a chauffeur. I knew what I was getting into and wondered how long I would be on this case. At Thomas Jefferson Hospital we were taught that from an ethical and professional point of view a nurse could never turn down a case. It turned out that I remained with the major until he died in June 1940.

When the major died, his wife, a former musician, went into shock and developed an enlarged heart. Again Dr. Rehfuss asked me if I would please stay with her. I really worked on that case! A hospital bed was set up, and several doctors were called in. One heart specialist said she could not live a week, but other physicians had different opinions. At any rate, a night nurse was engaged, and the two of us worked well together. It so happened that the patient lived

Approaching the Summit near Skyline.

for more than three years and enjoyed much that life had to offer.

Fortunately, Mrs. Beckurts had great determination to live. She enjoyed her friends, played the piano magnificently, and on Sundays various members of the Philadelphia Orchestra would visit her. Being with Mrs. Beckurts was an educational experience for me because she knew so many interesting people.

Now as I look back at my life I know that what happened next was an experience which provided the key piece and completed my life pattern up to that point.

Once Mrs. Beckurts had recovered sufficiently to travel, Dr. Rehfuss sent her to Frank Dodge's wonderful Mountain View House in Whitefield, New Hampshire. Margery Barger, the night nurse, and I accompanied her, and we quickly learned that she was quite at home there, since she and her family had been going to that hotel for years.

Up to that summer I had not done much traveling, as my nose had been to the grindstone most of the time. Therefore those two months in the White Mountains will never be forgotten. I enjoyed meeting Mrs. Beckurts's friends and playing bridge with them. It was almost a carefree vacation, and the freedom from giving intensive nursing care was unbelievable and relaxing. I thanked God many times for my blessings.

It was as though the sun had started to shine on my life. I had the opportunity for the first time to examine myself and consider what direction I should be taking from there on. Day after day I gazed across the fields and forests at Mount Washington and the other Presidentials from the Mountain View House, watching the green landscape gradually fade from its summer hue to the glorious colors of a New England autumn with snow on the crown of Mount Washington.

When we returned to Pennsylvania, Mrs. Beckurts wanted her two nurses to remain with her. Dr. Rehfuss was pleased, and I continued to give my patient the daily shots she required as well as her needed treatments. With this attention she remained in good spirits and health—and fortunately could afford the expense.

There was time for fun too. I loved attending the Friday afternoon concerts at the Academy of Music. Once we stopped off at Leopold Stokowski's home to pay him a visit. We often dined at the Union League Club, and my evenings were free for dating. My life pattern was certainly changing, and it was good.

Three of my dates still stand out in my memory above the others. I attended some AMA meetings and lectures with Dr. John Keithan but

THE CONSTRUCTION of the Cog Railway up Mount Washington was the commencement of a new era in steampower in overcoming grades over high mountain ascents. It opened new means of business enterprise and enlarged the facilities for enjoyment of the most beautiful scenery of the surrounding country.

During this construction, a Swiss engineer came to see Marsh and took away drawings of the machinery, the track, and the like, which were later used on a railway up Mount Rhigi in Switzerland. They used the center cograil, the peculiar feature of our Mount Washington Cog Railway. Thus, the United States of America has set an example worthy of imitation in an older country.

Looking across Jacob's Ladder toward Marshfield Station.

he wanted to marry me, so that he soon became too serious and I ended our dating. Pat Patterson dated me and also asked me to marry him, but I wasn't ready to settle down then, and besides, I didn't love him. Occasionally I traveled to New Canaan, Connecticut, to spend the weekend with Dr. Richard Barstow and his mother, father, and sister. We had good times together at the Litchfield Country Club where we would dine and dance, and we also enjoyed touring the countryside together.

In December 1940 Mrs. Beckurts, her daughter, Margery Barger, and I left for Miami Beach to stay at the Flamingo Hotel. Dr. Rehfuss felt that the climate there would be better and safer for our patient. We took the Atlantic Coast Line to Miami where her chauffeur was waiting for us and then drove us over the causeway to the hotel.

I had never been to Florida. It seemed like paradise just to listen to the sound of the whispering palms and inhale the scent of the rich wet earth. The hotel was situated right off Biscayne Bay where all the yachts tied up at the Flamingo dock. The cocktail lounge faced the water, and at that time of year there was usually spectacular sunsets.

Mrs. Beckurts always had her evening cocktail on the terrace which also overlooked the bay. It was an event to which we all looked forward and enjoyed. The four of us—Mrs. Beckurts, her daughter, Margery, and I—would relate the events of the day before we went into the huge dining room for dinner. Evenings we often spent in the beautifully furnished sitting room which opened off our bedrooms in Mrs. Beckurts's private suite.

Suddenly life seemed unreal. It seemed incredible that I was really living day after day in this dream world for which little was asked in return. We nurses would have our early breakfast in the dining room; then I would return to the suite and remain with our patient during most of the day. Margery was responsible for preparing Mrs. Beckurts for bed and for being "on the alert" all night should she be needed. It was not a very strenuous schedule for either of us!

"Lunchtime, girls!" Mrs. Beckurts would call, and the three of us would go down to her cabana where her daughter would join us. J. Edgar Hoover, the controversial FBI director, had his cabana next to ours. His radio played constantly and his bodyguard was ever present, which he told us he disliked. Since I always had my movie camera with me, I mustered up my courage one day and went over to his cabana.

"Mr. Hoover, would you do me a favor, please?" I asked. He

nodded graciously, having no idea what was coming next. "Would you mind walking toward me so I can take your picture?"

He smiled as he got to his feet. "That would be a pleasure, Miss Crawford, I'm sure you would make a good director."

The cabana beyond Mr. Hoover's was occupied by the young John Wanamakers of the John Wanamaker stores. They were part of the interesting crowd to which we belonged. These new friendships and the warm climate were good for our patient, and she seemed to thrive on them.

Evenings I double-dated with the Arthur Murray couple who taught dancing at the hotel, and we usually went to a night club, Palm Island being among our favorites. One of the performers we saw was Gypsy Rose Lee, who did her celebrated "striptease." I was surprised to find that the atmosphere was good and her act very refined and even artistic. In contrast, the Nut Club was on the vulgar side, but fun, and it was here I met "Kelly the Clown" who was a dreadful tease.

Sunset Over Biscayne Bay

Then came the evening of February 4, 1941.

"Ellen, I think I'll have my cocktail here in the sitting room tonight," Mrs. Beckurts said. She nodded in the direction of her daughter and the night nurse. "They thought they'd join me in here and you're welcome too, of course, but I thought you might like a chance to be free before dinner."

Never one to refuse an offer to be off and by myself, I thanked her. "I'll join you at the table at six-thirty," I promised, and a moment later I was hurrying toward the cocktail lounge where I took a small table facing Biscayne Bay.

"A martini—dry!" I told the waiter, half wondering what if anything might happen during this hour of liberty. I did not have to wait long to find out.

I had scarcely started sipping my drink when a large man who had the table next to ours in the dining room approached my table.

"May I join you for a drink?" he asked. "You look so lonely—and lovely too."

"Please do," I said, flattered at the attention of this older man. He was a huge powerful man who I judged was well over six feet tall and weighed at least 250 pounds. We introduced ourselves, and as we talked the sky slowly took on a gorgeous red hue.

"That's the most beautiful sunset I have ever seen," I half whispered.

There was a short pause before he replied. Then he contradicted me. "No, you have never seen a sunset until you have seen one from the top of Mount Washington."

I looked at him astonished. "Mount Washington, New Hampshire?"

"Of course."

"Why, I was looking over from the Mountain View House at the peak every day late this summer. Isn't that a coincidence!"

"Then promise me the next time you come up to New Hampshire you'll visit me at the base." He went on to explain that he owned the Mount Washington Cog Railway and that his name was Henry Teague but was called Colonel Teague.

"My manager's joining me tomorrow," he said. "He has the same last name as mine—but we're not related. He's Arthur. I'd like you to meet him."

"Thank you," I said with as much enthusiasm as I could muster. I was thinking of my date for that evening, and the prospect of meeting another older man who undoubtedly talked about nothing but trains hardly excited me.

How wrong I was to be!

"Base Station" on Jacob's Ladder.

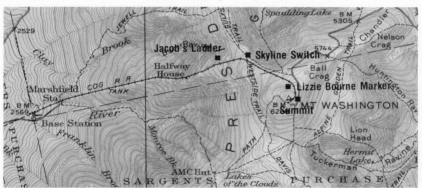

$\mathcal{S}$ UDDENLY *Ellen Teague was aware that the car had pitched forward somewhat, a sure signal that they were approaching Jacob's Ladder—that incredible part of the track which had the steepest grade of any railroad in the world. She remembered her first ride on the Cog Railway when she wondered whether the little engine actually would be able to push the passenger car up this almost vertical rise. Again, on the down trip, she worried lest the engine not be able to keep from running away—unaware then that the locomotive and the coach had their own independent braking systems. All went well on that trip, however, as it always had, and as she knew it would today.*

"Ladies and gentlemen," the conductor was announcing, "for the benefit of any passengers who have just joined us, we are now on the highest trestle on the road and—incidentally—it can also be the windiest place on the railroad. Our grade here is over 37 percent. If you look off to

your left, you can make out the Lakes-of-the-Clouds Hut of the Appalachian Mountain Club there above the skyline. Thank you."

Jacob's Ladder—Ellen knew the statistics by heart! The grade here is 37.41 percent or a rise of 1,980 feet per mile, which she realized means little until one sits in the coach and sees how very steep this part of the track is. It would have been interesting if the conductor had mentioned also that the trestle had been named for the nearby steep craig which hung over the deep Ammonoosuc Ravine. It must have been a religious person who had taken the name from the story of Jacob's dream of a ladder extending up to heaven.

Curious, Ellen recalled, how Jacob's Ladder provided another piece in her life's pattern. Four years before she had met Arthur and Colonel Teague, the famous 1938 hurricane had slammed into New England and roared up through the White Mountains, pushing over everything in its path. Although it spared the Mount Washington summit buildings, its full force was felt just below within the four-to five-thousand-foot level of the mountain where it savagely twisted and then demolished Jacob's Ladder and a half mile of trestle. The Colonel rebuilt the track at a cost of $60,000 and five weeks later trains were running safely again. What a contrast, Ellen thought, $60,000 to fix just the trestle when the total cost of building the railroad initially was only a little over twice that amount!

She smiled, thinking how the hurricane had triggered the chain of events which followed. To obtain the money needed for the repairs, the Colonel had asked his alma mater, Dartmouth College, for a loan, and because the administration had responded at a time when it was difficult to borrow money, the grateful Colonel willed the railroad to the college. Ten years after his death in 1952, the college offered to sell the road to Arthur, and that was how the Cog Railway remained with Teagues—even though the men were not related. Funny how things work out—the Colonel—Arthur and then Ellen Teague . . .

44

4

Arthur Teague

THE NEXT EVENING, true to his promise, Colonel Teague came over to our table at dinner.

"Miss Crawford, I'd like you to meet my manager, this is Arthur Teague," he said.

My first impression of this man was not pleasing, although to be honest I had not thought about him again since the Colonel mentioned him the previous evening at cocktails. Arthur Simpson Teague was of average height, and what struck me forcefully at first was how ugly he was. A large birthmark extended across his nose and seemed to disfigure what otherwise would have been a rather pleasant face. I did find his steady hazel eyes attractive, however, and when we shook hands there was something electrifying about his firm but gentle grip.

"If you're not busy would you care to go dancing tonight?" he asked, taking me somewhat by surprise. In spite of the nose (which I soon discovered was not so ugly after all), I felt flattered at the invitation, and that proved the first of several dates before he left on a business trip. He said that he would appreciate seeing me when he returned from Mexico, and I told him by all means to get in touch with me.

Arthur was born and raised in Graniteville, South Carolina, attended Richmond Academy in Augusta, Georgia, and then entered Clemson University. After graduation he worked for the South Carolina Power and Light Company before accepting a job on the Mount Washington Cog Railway, of which he soon became manager. He was three years older than I, and we seemed to have many interests in common. He was kind and considerate and always acted as a gentleman, which was important to me.

While Arthur was away Mrs. Beckurts, her daughter, the night nurse, and I had a marvelous time. We went frequently to the races at Hialeah Park, attended jai alai games, visited the famous Bird Farm, watched the trained porpoises perform, saw Clyde Beatty and his trained lions, and seemed to be on the go every moment. This full schedule appeared to be good for our patient—to say nothing of her nurses—and in no time it was the end of February and Arthur was back. On our first date he told me he was joining the army on March 17.

"Will you keep in touch with me, Ellen?" he asked, those hazel eyes staring into mine with what I sensed was more than an ordinary bit of interest.

"You know I will, Art," I replied, and he reached across the table to clasp my hand within his.

Meanwhile, Pat Patterson had become more attentive than ever, sending a barrage of registered letters to Whitefield and now to Miami Beach. I was also corresponding with Arthur, whom I now called Art.

Our Romance Grows

In April we four ladies returned to Philadelphia, and again Mrs. Beckurts asked Margery and me to stay with her. The end of June found us back in the Mountain View House with its spectacular view of Mount Washington, but now the sight had a new meaning to me. It

MORE AND MORE people are visiting Mount Washington and riding the Cog Railway to its summit. The railway has made it possible for all ages to enjoy its uniqueness. Close to 250,000 people now reach the summit one way or another each season. This is almost one third of New Hampshire's entire population. Mount Washington commands one of the finest views of any mountain in America. It is the most important tourist attraction in New Hampshire, and possibly northern New England.

Arthur S. Teague.

was further enhanced when I received a letter from Art saying he had a leave and would be heading for the base of Mount Washington.

"My visit will be short," he wrote, "but I want to see you and spend as much time with you as you can spare."

Mrs. Beckurts enthusiastically agreed with Margery's offer to cover for me so that I could spend as much time as I wished with my new friend. I was decidedly mixed up, not being sure how I felt toward either Pat or Art but knowing I must wait and not hurry any decisions.

The minute Art reached the Base Station at Mount Washington he must have headed directly for the phone booth and called me. That night he took me to the Moon Room at the Mount Washington Hotel in Bretton Woods. This proved a romantic evening for me and I suspect was somewhat of a turning point in our relationship. The next day we rode the Cog together, having lamb chops before leaving the base and finishing with dessert on the summit! Coming down we rode on the platform, and I was so excited I did not notice the soot in my hair until I had returned to the hotel. Art and I had dinner together, and during the evening he told me that he had to return to his post the following day. Next morning I went down to the Whitefield railroad station to say another goodbye as his train made a scheduled stop there. I ran down the platform and found the car where he was standing on the steps just as the train started moving. When we waved and called goodbye, I think both of us realized then that we cared for each other deeply.

As that summer of 1941 slipped away the war clouds slowly rolled up, and once I was back in Philadelphia I was recruited by the Jefferson Hospital Nursing Unit to train in Texas whenever the army might send for us. While waiting I stayed on with Mrs. Beckurts, and just before we were to leave for Miami Beach, Pat came to ask for my decision. I promised him an answer by April if my unit had not left by then and if I knew how I felt about Art.

Several weeks after we had settled down in the same suite in the Flamingo Hotel, Art asked me to come to Columbus, Georgia, for a dance at the club and "a talk." I took several of Pat's letters with me which I had not had time to read—let alone open. It was an exciting weekend, my first experience with men in uniform, and when Sunday night came I knew I had decided between Art and Pat. Without opening the letters, I threw them into the wastepaper basket.

At the station as I prepared to board the train, Art held out his fraternity pin.

"Ellen, dear, I want you to wear this. You know what it means?"

I nodded and tears came to my eyes. "Oh, Art!" was all I could say. He put his arms around me and hugged me tightly, and he just had time to put the pin on my coat and give me a kiss before the conductor ordered me aboard.

"How soon can we get married?" he asked as I started up the steps.

I turned. "Just give me a few months, Art, to see if I should get married or stay with my unit when we're called up."

The train was moving now, and I was so happy and thrilled it seems as though I must have cried all the way back to Miami Beach!

Interim

A month later Art came to see me, and after we discussed our plans I notified the Jefferson Unit that I would not be going with them to Texas. Art made it quite clear that he wanted me to be with him and that "one was enough in the army."

That spring I served as the Phillies's mascot while they were training at Flamingo Park, a different experience which got my picture in the newspapers. Meanwhile, Art was fifteen miles from Columbus, Georgia, with the Fourth Motorized Division. He was fortunate because he was in a good temporary wood barracks with hot-air heat and one officer to a room, whereas some of the men were cramped three men to a tent.

Art kept me informed wherever he went. It was very thoughtful of him, and I was thrilled to know and be in love with such a wonderful man. The training he and his men were receiving was intense, and his letters brought the war very close to me. After describing an especially intensive two-day maneuver, he finished his letter, writing:

Sure did think about you and wish you were here when I was eating dinner at the officers club. You see on Sunday night they have a buffet dinner and dancing. First time I've seen an evening dress since I saw that pretty white one of yours in Miami. Glad you liked the roses. Wished I could have dropped in on you but Uncle Sam just won't let us run around. Received orders from Regimental Hdqrs. to start checking the company property as Capt. Sharp is being sent to Jacksonville, Florida. So this boy will be busy next week—and the whippoorwill is sounding off—so nite, nite, love "Art."

Every time I opened Art's letters I tingled all over with dread and expectancy because, although he kept me well posted, I never knew what would happen. I have never shared these letters with anyone until now, and his next note contained the inevitable news:

It was only a week ago that they requested all officers and men straighten out their affairs at home and be prepared to move on a moment's notice. They even sent out a blank form asking if our wills were filed, our bank accounts kept, and did we own a cemetery lot. Starting last Saturday, the medical department started giving tetanus shots to all the men and officers. I took tetanus, typhoid and small pox all last Saturday—gee it was a nice weekend!

Both of us realized that there was little time before he would be leaving for the war front, and we decided to act before it was too late.

Engagement and Marriage

In April 1942 my brother-in-law, Jack Morgan, announced our engagement to some thirty friends gathered in our Philadelphia home at 417 South Carlisle Street. It was a happy occasion for Art and me. Art arrived with a beautiful bunch of arbutus, which had a special meaning for us.

Following our engagement we made arrangements to be married at Saint Paul's Church in Augusta, Georgia, on June 6, 1942. That site was preferable to Philadelphia since Art would not be able to get a long enough leave from the service to make a wedding in Philadelphia practicable. Mother, my sister Jane, and I took the Southern Railway to Augusta, arriving several days before the wedding. We were met at the station by a few of the officers' wives and taken to the Partridge Inn.

The weather was hot, but the smell of magnolia blossoms filled my room, brought in by the gentle breezes through the large open window, this being before the era of air conditioning! Our day to become one arrived sooner than I had anticipated. That afternoon we were both so nervous we couldn't find the license, but it finally turned up and we were only a half hour late for our service!

It was a lovely wedding. We were married by the Reverend Hamilton West who later became bishop of Florida. Mother gave me away, and Jane was my maid of honor. Uncle Henry (the Colonel) was Art's best man. Art's mother and his sister Lucy, her husband, Dr. Charles Bullock, and their son Claude and daughter Betty arrived for the affair. In addition, several colonels, majors, captains, and their wives were present. After the ceremony the families went to the Forrest Hotel for our wedding supper.

Art and I had two days for our wedding trip to Charleston, South Carolina, where we stayed at the Fort Sumter Hotel. On our return to the Partridge Inn in Augusta, I found that I seemed to fit nicely with the army wives; we got along well together. Colonel Van Fleet and his wife had the room next to Art's and mine. We were prepared for "alerts" and told to be ready to move anytime. Many of our evenings were spent out at Camp Gordon with our husbands. We were permitted to know a little of what was going on and told to be cautious with whom we talked. All of us felt committed and ready for action, if need be. We knitted sweaters, socks, scarfs, helmetliners, and blankets.

I had been married just a short time when Art was told he would be gone on maneuvers for three to four weeks. I decided to head north for

New Hampshire to be with my former patient, who was not too well. Mrs. Beckurts had asked me to return to her if I had any time.

Soon after Art left for maneuvers, I took the train from Augusta back to the White Mountains. I was so glad I returned to help, as Mrs. Beckurts needed blood transfusions and care and she was most grateful to me. I was with her only a little over two weeks when she started hemorrhaging. We could not save her, and it was very sad to part with such a very wonderful person.

I went to Cincinnati with her daughter, Isabel, for the burial. We then returned to New Hampshire, and I was there just three days when Art called to say that he was in South Carolina and to see what connections I could make to return to him.

I traveled from Whitefield to New York on a night train, which came in at Grand Central Station, and taxied over to Pennsylvania Station several minutes before there was a blackout. I wandered in the dark for a bit before I remembered I had a small flashlight in my bag. Somehow I managed to find a ticket window and got the last overnight Pullman to Florence, South Carolina. It was heavenly to be back in my husband's arms. I could tell he was as glad as I, for we were extremely sensitive to each other's feelings.

August and September soon passed with many scares as to where Art would go next and what type of training would be required —there was always an alert feeling that our husbands could be called to the port of embarkation. That was the way it was in the army.

I became pregnant sometime in October and remember Art saying that made him feel good "because now he knew he was a man." At first I didn't know if I wanted to start a family because of the war and our traveling, but Art seemed to want a child, so I said to myself, "Here goes." One's first pregnancy, I found, is sort of a challenge to see if one can continue doing all one has done previously, including one of our favorite pastimes, dancing.

The conga was the dance during my World War II years. I always loved to lead the conga at the army dances and was able to keep going with the crowd. Our first Christmas together at camp was different from any I had ever experienced. The officers and their wives got together and had a holiday dance at the Forrest Hotel.

By the time January came around I had made Art a sweater (khaki color, of course), a scarf, and two pairs of wool khaki stockings which were done on round needles to make the stockings fit comfortably in his boots. Then I started a woolen helmet, a cap which comes down over the neck and onto the shoulders, to be worn on the battlefield under the steel helmet. Some of the other wives made these but there were many who didn't and I know Art appreciated it because he knew he would need the wool liner overseas.

The early part of 1943 the Fourth Motorized was told it was going to Fort Dix. None of us knew what the war plans were, but everyone was alerted, and off we went to New Jersey. Four of the officers and their wives took over Mirrorbank, an old inn near Fort Dix, Art and I being one of the couples. We drew straws for rooms, and each family set up its own eating table at the lodge. Since there was a huge cooking range in the kitchen, there was plenty of space for all of us to be able to cook our individual meals. I was able to scrape up some curtains for the dining room, and it soon became quite homelike.

I was getting heavier with my pregnancy but kept going. Art, now a lieutenant colonel, had to attend many officers' classes during the evenings. After several months at Fort Dix, some of the officers were notified that they were to attend the assault course at Fort Belvoir, Virginia. Art was one of them, and as the baby would be due soon, I decided to return to Philadelphia where I could be near my doctor, Dr. John Montgomery, who was to deliver my baby.

June was very hot, but I'm sure Art was even warmer at Fort Belvoir. It was difficult carrying the baby, and I hoped that he or she would be coming before too long because I wished to be back with Art as long as I could before he left for overseas.

Dear friends of mine, the Wagners, invited me out to Paoli for the Fourth of July. I hesitated but at the last minute decided to go. During that night I felt changes and on the morning of July 6 decided to return home to be near the Jefferson Hospital and my doctor. I felt very uncomfortable and knew that the miracle I had witnessed so often as a nurse would soon be given to me. My membranes broke on July 7 and I went into the hospital. Around 5:00 P.M. I delivered a darling baby girl through a breach delivery; the baby was small and there were no problems. My sister Jane remained through the delivery and then wired Art immediately. I named my little girl after my sister Jane.

In the meantime, Art had been transferred back to Fort Benning, Georgia, where he was taking all the officers' tests he could and scored "excellent" on each. He was off to a good start, not that he was trying to make good grades, but he wanted to know everything necessary for a commander in combat, since he realized its importance to his men.

Rotogravure photo of "Socialite Ellen Crawford offering feminine competition for the Phillies."

He hoped to finish this course at Fort Benning before going overseas, and every day there were rumors—as always!

I had little Jane baptized at Saint Thomas Church in Whitemarsh two weeks after she was born. Then I made plans to catch a train to Atlanta so I could join Art. I bought a bassinet and decided to travel light and nurse the baby as long as I could to save making formulas while traveling in the service. Art took the bus to Atlanta to meet us. There he was on the platform, his eyes eagerly searching each window as the train slowed for its stop. He saw me and ran alongside our car, then jumped aboard and pushed his way through the line of passengers waiting to get off.

"Ellen!" he cried, and when he saw the baby he removed his cap, leaned down, and kissed first me and then Janie. I shall never forget the tender, loving expression as he looked at our little child for the first time, oblivious to the crowd about us.

Art had gotten me a room not too far from the post with a family who had a small child, so all worked out for the time being. Art was

with me as much as possible during the evenings. At last Art completed his tests and told me he felt now he would be ready when called
to care for his men.

In September our next stop was Apalachicola on the Gulf of Mexico
for training in amphibious landing on the French coast. Like the other
wives, I lived in a fishing village and drove back and forth at least forty
miles each way to be with Art. Some nights I stayed in the barracks,
sleeping with Art in his army cot while Janie slept in his footlocker. It
was well worth the effort for the three of us to be together. We didn't
know how long all this would last, but I was determined to do my part.

After two months of amphibious training we packed up and went
to Virginia Beach for more courses, and finally in December our last
post was Fort Jackson in Columbia, South Carolina, where Cousin
Mary Swearingen was able to get us a modern and cozy apartment.
We spent Christmas and the New Year together, but as we moved into
mid-January everyone became tense. We knew now—any moment.

One evening when Art returned home he was so quiet that I sensed
something was wrong. After supper he leaned back in his chair,
stared at the floor, and said: "This is it. We leave at three in the
morning for the port of embarkation."

For a moment I froze. Although I thought I had prepared myself for
this moment, I wasn't ready. It was a dreadful night, one I shall never
forget. I turned on every light in the apartment at two o'clock, determined that it would be bright for my Art. When he left I stood in the
doorway until I knew he could no longer see me.

After that awful separation it seemed time stood still. I went
through the motions of caring for Janie, preparing simple meals for
myself, and keeping the apartment clean. Then about a week later the
phone rang. It was my first cousin, Admiral John Grabel Crawford,
called Dick, calling from Philadelphia. Dick had stopped in to see my
mother and sister Jane.

"Ellen," he said, "Cousin Homer Grunninger—he's in charge of
the port of embarkation in New York—he just called to say he saw in
the orders that Art's coming and will have three days before he ships
overseas. What would you like to do?"

What would I like to do? What would any wife and mother want to
do? See her husband again, of course! I immediately called Art's
mother to ask if she too would like to see Art again before he left and if
so to take the bus from Greenville to Columbia, South Carolina, and
be ready to leave with me early in the morning. We would have to

drive straight through if we were to make it to Philadelphia in time to see Art.

"I'll be waiting at the bus terminal at seven o'clock, Ellen," was her quick reply, "and bless you for thinking of me, too."

I had four retread tires, no spare, and barely enough ration stamps to buy gas, as I had tried to save them for such an emergency. I packed the car that evening and met Mother Teague next morning as agreed. We put little Janie between us and set out for the most taxing drive I have ever taken. That night we were stopped time and again as we went through towns which had blackouts. While we waited for permission to proceed I would nurse Janie, then off we would go again.

I was about three months pregnant and getting so tired as we approached Washington, D.C., that I stopped to call my mother. Dick Crawford answered, reassured me all would be well, and urged me to take it easy the rest of the way. I asked if my sister Jane could take the train to Washington and drive us home. We met her at the Union Station, and I will always be grateful to Jane for what she did.

Art was scheduled to arrive in Philadelphia that night and would come over to Mother's house. I didn't know what would be left of me by then, but I forgot my fatigue when the doorbell rang.

"Quick! Hide in the living room!" Jane pushed Mother Teague and me in behind the door as she and Dick went to the front hall. After a short greeting they brought Art into the living room, and when he saw us he rushed up and squeezed me so hard I was afraid I might lose the new baby. He was so happy, so very happy he almost cried.

When Art left early next morning, this time his face reflected peace and gratitude. As he stood in the doorway and kissed me, he whispered, "I'll return to you, Ellen, I promise, and I'll be in touch just as soon as I can." Then he was gone—this time for good.

Several weeks after Art left I was invited to a party at Cassy Staples' home in Penllyn. I really didn't feel like joining the merry crowd and said so, but my sister Marnie insisted that I go. Shortly after I arrived I felt the tears mounting, and I escaped upstairs to cry alone as I thought of Art. I could not stand the merriment without him and left. Parties were no longer for me; I belonged home with Janie.

I will share one of Art's letters written while at sea.

My dear Ellen,
Another day at sea has gone. I get around to my troops about twice a day. It is a beautiful sight to stand up on the top deck and look out at the convoy.

The Waumbek engine and Chumley coach at Jacob's Ladder.

Just to take a good look gives you quite a bit of confidence. No one is worrying about the trip—to most of my men it is just another change of station,—and the favorite pastime is cards—dice, one of ship's crew said this was the darndest outfit he ever saw. It is almost a Monte Carlo. I have not joined any of the games. I do have to tell you to take care of Ellen—please, with all my love,

"*Art*"

    I corresponded with many of the officers' wives, and we kept asking ourselves when the scenes would change overseas. By this time I was not feeling too well with my second pregnancy and was experiencing problems with bleeding. I had done too much during the early months, but I guess God wanted it this way and I certainly put my faith and trust in him, no matter what was to happen, and that is all I could do.

    Meanwhile, Art had arrived safely in England. He was training out on the moors and enjoying the lovely countryside.

    As I write these remembrances and review Art's letters, I realize how much of our lives we shared with each other, and how much

closer we became even through our wartime censored correspondence.

One day a letter of Art's enclosed a note from Henry Teague. It
read:

My dear Arthur:
I got your post card from the government and know that you are on the way
for your great adventure and what you have been training for for two and
one-half years. As you know I have undoubted faith in the goodness of God
and know you are going to return safe into the arms of your family.
I am stayng in bed ten hours a day, endeavoring to cure the strain on my
heart in order that I can keep the railway for you when you do come back. A
lot of people want that road, as you know, but I think I have it fixed alright.
I wrote to Ellen today and hope that your mother will be with her some
time. I understand that the Mount Washington Hotel is going to open next
summer. If so I am going to open my cabins, whether I open the railway or
not. Remember your first steamboat ride on the Belfast to Boston?
                                              Love
                                              Henry N. Teague

Uncle Henry Teague surely was a character, and he loved Art very
much. It never bothered Art a bit that everyone used to call him Uncle
Henry's "man Friday."

I was having more trouble now with my pregnancy. Dr. Montgomery prescribed bed for me and I stayed there most of the time, but as
April passed into May I knew I would lose the baby. I guess it was for
the best. Dr. John Montgomery delivered the lovely little boy baby
and said, "No fees, Ellen, for I wish to contribute my services to this
part of my warwork." The baby was stillborn. I left his little body in
the laboratory for study, hoping it would someday save another
infant.

D Day at Last!

As the days dragged on my anxiety grew. No news, no news, and I
felt that our men had gone into battle somewhere. On June 6 I had an
appointment with Dr. Montgomery and mentioned my intuitive feeling that they had "gone over." That same afternoon I heard the boys
shouting "Extra! Extra!" as they came down the street with newspap-

The "family" before Art went overseas.

ers proclaiming D day. Now the radio was hysterically telling about the invasion, and I sat there hour after hour listening—wondering —and praying. I knew there was nothing I could do except wait, and wait I did.

The news I was waiting for was told in the June 20, 1944, issue of *Stars and Stripes,* and I quote part of the article:

One regiment of the Fourth hit the beaches at H-hour on D-Day with the other two following an hour or so later. Theirs was the unenviable mission of scrambling through the marshland flooded by the Jerries before the enemy backed up from the coastal zone on the west side of the peninsula. The Third Battalion of another regiment, commanded by Lt. Colonel Arthur S. Teague, had to advance four miles through these inundated areas, most of the time up to their hips in mud and water. They made such rapid progress against these odds that some of the units closed with retreating Germans to engage them in hand-to-hand combat.

How proud I was that my wonderful husband had come through the landing! He told me later that it would have been a sorry sight without the marines who backed the troops. The marines, God bless them!

Art's regiment was cited:

On D-Day Colonel Teague commanded the first 1500 men to land on Utah Beach and led them four miles through German lines to join paratroop forces, where they fought for nine consecutive days and nights. For this action, Teague's battalion won the Presidential Unit Citation for extraordinary heroism and outstanding performance of duty in action in Normandy, France.

In deference to Art's modesty and unselfish devotion to his country, I shall merely relate that he was wounded, sent to England for treatment and rest, and then returned to the Continent "to finish the job," as he put it. He dismissed the fact that he received, among other awards, the French Croix de Guerre, the British Distinguished Service Order, the Silver Star, the Bronze Star, and the Purple Heart. "It is not the medal, but the idea which counts."

Meanwhile I had been living with mother, but during the summer of 1945 I rented a small cottage at Hyannis Port on Cape Cod. Art and I

Mt. Washington from the Base.

had always shared our lives with our families, and they needed our love and support as much as we needed theirs. We both tried to do what we felt was right because of all our parents had done for us. For this reason I had invited both our mothers to spend the summer with Janie and me at this cottage.

One day during July I received a most unexpected phone call.

Art's Return

"Ellen—Ellen—is that you?" My heart seemed to stop.

"Art!" was all I could say.

"Oh, Ellen! It's so wonderful to hear your voice and . . ."

"Where are you, dear?" I interrupted, so excited I hardly knew what I was saying.

"I'm at your house—in Philadelphia and . . ."

"Then you didn't get my letter telling you where I am?"

"No—I came straight here and they told me where you are. How's

Janie? Oh—I can't wait to see you, I'll come on the first train and . . ."

At last our long wait was over! But as I thought of tomorrow I had mixed emotions of anxiety and elation. I tried to imagine how Art would look and how he would act. How would I appear to him after a year and a half? Would we pick up again where we had left off?

And so it was that the next morning three women and one two-year-old child representing three generations were waiting eagerly on the Hyannis platform for the train from New York. We heard a whistle, and Janie's fingers tightened about mine.

"Noise?" she asked anxiously.

I kneeled beside her. "That's Daddy's train," I said, and two minutes later we were in his arms. There were tears streaming from all eyes, and garbled words of greeting were exchanged back and forth as first one and then the other greeted and hugged him. Poor Janie was confused and momentarily forgotten in the excitement, but Art quickly picked her up and hugged and loved the bewildered little girl until I realized that she needed her mother's reassurance and took her from him.

That evening as we drove alone to the edge of the shore and looked up at a full moon, I knew that my wonderings about our reunion had been groundless. I felt we had never been separated—all through the war we had supported each other spiritually and had looked forward confidently to being reunited—and here we were sitting by the water's edge in the bright moonlight. Later we fell into each other's arms with a single sigh, this being our first night together in eighteen months. I believe that Margaret Ellen Teague, our second little girl, was blessed with life that night. I said a prayer of gratitude before I fell asleep.

After two weeks on the Cape we drove to North Carolina where Art spent the balance of his active service, retiring early in the spring of 1946 but remaining in the Reserves. At the same time he applied to the University of Virginia Law School and was accepted for its accelerated course. It seemed our future was taking shape as we drove to Charlottesville and bought our first property where we planned an apartment house with four units, hoping to live in one of them ourselves. Our second daughter, Margaret Ellen, was born on April 19, 1946. She weighed eight pounds and seven ounces, a welcome addition to our little family.

Art did well at law school and continued his studies into the spring of 1947. We were enjoying Charlottesville and looking forward to summer when Uncle Henry unexpectedly came back into our lives.

Riding down Jacob's Ladder toward Midpoint on the devil's shingle.

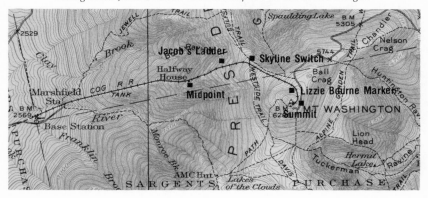

*T*HE TRAIN *had reached the midpoint of its journey and here the track seemed level compared with the steep grade of Jacob's Ladder. The steady metallic noise produced by the engine and coach made Ellen think back to Walter Aiken, the machinist and inventor who became Sylvester Marsh's manager as well as the largest individual stockholder of the new road. She enjoyed recalling how Aiken had been responsible for perfecting Marsh's inventions and adapting them to practical use on the railway because it always made her think of another manager—her Art. Perhaps this was why she had such a warm feeling for Aiken.*

She smiled at the recollection of the time Aiken was up at the summit ready to ride the train and something went wrong with the locomotive. He donned overalls, dived underneath to fix the trouble, and then took a seat in

63

the coach. A passenger sitting nearby who had seen him emerge from under the engine called to him.

"My good man, would you please bring me a drink of water? I'm afraid I'll lose my seat if I get out."

Aiken, thoughtful of others and their comfort, and not unmindful of the humor of the situation, procured water in a tin dipper and handed it to the woman, who presently drank it. The incident would have closed here, but to show her appreciation the woman proceeded to hand Aiken a modest tip.

Not in the least disturbed, but with perfect self-possession, Aiken remarked: "Madam, I've put a good deal of money and time into this railroad, and this is the first dividend I've seen. It's so small I don't think I'd better take it." With that he turned away.

Turning to the brakeman who had just arrived, the startled woman gasped, "Who is that strange man?"

"Why, that's Mr. Aiken who built the railway," was his reply.

The recollection of this event never ceased to amuse Ellen, but there was also an added thrill, for it reminded her of Arthur Teague, that later manager who was as inventive and clever as Aiken, his predecessor. Now, at sunset, it was almost as though Art was sitting there beside her on this, her last trip. Much had happened since his death, and in her heart she hoped he would have approved of everything she had done to keep their railroad running.

With these thoughts she became aware again of the slight rhythm in the car's movement, and she felt Art's presence too. Arthur Simpson Teague . . .

64

5

Digging in at the Base

ART RETURNED from his class on contracts and agreements. "Ellen," he called as he opened the front door, "a letter from Uncle Henry—he wants me to come back as general manager!"

The expression on his face betrayed his excitement and the inner conflict he was experiencing. "There's a big job to be done," he continued as he glanced at the sheet, "track has to be rebuilt, employees found again, equipment checked out." He looked up at me and nodded his head slowly. "Sure would be a challenge. I could almost be tempted!"

That night we lay awake late discussing the pros and cons. Here he was studying law and looking forward to a successful and lucrative practice to support his growing family. He was thoroughly enjoying his classes and the long hours of reading and studying required, but he was an engineer at heart and an engineer by training. The prospect of running that little railroad up and down Mount Washington was exciting, and Uncle Henry's bid was flattering. It meant leaving law school before the end of the semester for something that had immediacy, something that needed him, and something he knew and loved. Continuing his law studies called for one more year at the university and then the usual years of clerking and assisting before he would be considered a full-fledged attorney.

"Tell me truthfully, Ellen," he said for the third time, "are you sure you want me to chuck the law for the railroad?"

Henry Nelson Teague at the Flamingo Hotel.

Again I explained that what I wanted most of all was for him to be happy in his work. As for me, I had to confess that the thought of going up to Mount Washington to live and bring up the family had definite nostalgia and appeal. I remembered vividly that day I took my one and only ride up the railway with Art—when we ate lamb chops at the base and dessert at the summit—the night before we both realized that we were serious about each other.

"Yes, Art, I would love to follow you up there, be part of the team that keeps that railroad running. I think we've both decided that railroading is in our blood and legal briefs are not!"

Colonel Henry N. Teague

To understand Art's decision, it is necessary to digress to present additional information about Colonel Henry N. Teague, who was the owner and president of the railroad for twenty years. I should like to quote from the late F. Allen Burt's *The Story of Mount Washington:*

Almost everyone who has much to do with Mount Washington sets up some sort of record. If he has color in his make-up and a love for the rough, tough old mountain, then he is almost sure to do something that marks him as a record-maker. Of such was the late Colonel Henry Nelson Teague, one of

MANY BOOKS and articles have been written about Mount Washington and the Cog Railway. To mark the publication of Frank Allen Burt's *The Story of Mount Washington,* Art and I gave a luncheon for him in the old Summit House, which has since been torn down.

Allen Burt was a well-known Boston writer, teacher, and advertising executive whose grandfather and later his father edited and published the famous *Among the Clouds* newspaper on the top of Mount Washington. When he died Allen left all of his *Among the Clouds* papers to a Boston museum.

Allen Burt's three grandsons worked summers for the Cog Railway and one of them married Janie's classmate, Cathy Holt.

Passengers on the B&M coach pose at Fabyan, September 14, 1906.

the colorful characters connected with the Mount Washington Railway, and its owner and president for 20 years.

Henry Teague was a big man, over six feet tall and large in proportion, who planned things in a big way and put his plans into operation. Nobody else has done more to further travel to the summit and to make possible year-round scientific research on the mountain.

By 1931 the cog railway had become a very unpopular stepchild of the Boston & Maine Railroad. Running less than three months a year, and showing no profit, the problem of maintenance and of building each year an operating personnel had become a job which no official of B. & M. wanted to tackle.

So President Edward S. French of the B. & M. delegated his assistant, Laurence F. Whittemore, to get rid of the mountain railroad. Mr. Whittemore was a man who carried things through. During the next 20 years he became in turn the president of the Federal Reserve Bank of Boston, of the New York, New Haven & Hartford Railroad, and of the Brown Company, the great papermaking firm of Berlin, New Hampshire, and Portland, Maine.

Mr. Whittemore went to see Colonel William A. Barron of the Crawford House and said: "Billy, Mr. French and the directors of the B. & M. have decided to sell the Mount Washington Railway. He wants you to get together a group of White Mountain hotel men to buy the railway and operate it. We will make the price and terms to suit you. Will you do it?"

Colonel Barron said: "Whit, I appreciate your coming to me with this offer, and I will give you my answer now." He paused for a moment, grasping the arms of his desk chair even more firmly, "My answer is 'No!' I have enough troubles of my own in the hotel business without taking on a railroad! What you need is a circus promoter; a man who can run the road, increase services, stir up business, publicize the railway to get more people interested in taking the trip up Mount Washington."

Later, Mr. Whittemore came again to Colonel Barron with this news: "We are making progress along those lines you mentioned. We have contacted Henry N. Teague, and we believe we have interested him. What do you think of him for the job?"

"Good!" replied Colonel Barron. "Henry is a real promoter. And he has energy enough to do the job as it should be done."

So the officials of the railroad and Henry N. Teague sat down and talked. Together they worked out what seemed like an almost grotesque conclusion—one man to buy a railroad, even a three-and-a-quarter mile railroad, and force it to pay a profit when a great system like the Boston & Maine saw nothing in it but hard work and headaches.

But the oldest mountain climbing cog railway in the world is no commonplace venture. And the man whose booming voice came to outdo the puffing of his funny little engines was no ordinary individual. Indeed, a man who could buy a railroad for $100,000—all on a mortgage—could not be "ordinary" in any sense of the word.

In the days of the Florida land boom of the twenties, Henry Teague was doing all right, until everything seemed to fall apart. Then, as he told a reporter in Miami, "I dropped about $1,000,000 down here." When the B. & M. officials asked him to take over the railroad, the hotel on the top, and all the land and the buildings at the base as well as the whole summit of the mountain, he told them he was broke, so they said they'd take his note. He said he didn't have money for operating expenses, so they put $10,000 in the bank for him.

Perhaps nobody but Henry Teague could have so successfully merged his personality and his life with this railroad and made of it "one of the world's most unique, interesting, and thrilling recreational attractions." Certainly it was only a man of his vision and exceptional courage who could have weathered those first few years, when equipment, untrained personnel, and foul weather posed continuous problems that had to be met day after

Train crew in the early 1920s during B&M ownership of the Cog.

day. But there were days of sunshine when crowds began to respond to his
publicity. And there were men who built themselves into the organization,
to return spring after spring to form the core of what is now a smooth-
running group of seasoned railroaders.

Teague had never before been in the railroad business. Born on Mt. Desert
Island, Maine, June 2, 1875, he was graduated from Dartmouth in 1900,
and was the first graduate from its Amos Tuck School of Finance in 1901.
He took time out from college to serve as a private in Company E, First New
Hampshire Volunteers, during the Spanish-American War.

Story has it that, when talking over the cog railway, he met with Colonel
Barron and Governor John Winant of New Hampshire at the Crawford
House. Billy Barron made some humorous comment on the fact that he was
a colonel while Henry had served as a private. Thereupon the Governor
said, "I will fix that," and appointed Teague to his staff with the rank of
colonel.

Business on the railroad was stimulated by the driving force of Henry
Teague's continuous supervision and contagious enthusiasm. "Big, busy,
and brusque," was one writer's description of the man. Sometimes it was

difficult to see the difference between his brusqueness, and what might have been termed bad temper. Once when someone hailed him with: "How are you, Colonel Teague?" his rejoinder was, "Just as cross as ever!"

But anyone who saw what he was up against in changing the old schedule of two trains a day to "A train every hour on the hour," training college boys and teachers, and in bucking weather that drove people away from the mountain, would agree that his occasional outbursts of wrath were not without provocation. Many a time during his first years with the railway he would sit on a piazza overlooking the base, wrapped in a huge overcoat, a big cap pulled down close over his shaggy brows (a cigar clenched between his powerful jaws, the ashes inching out unnoticed to fall finally over the overcoat), apparently miles away with some knotty problem, but keeping a watchful eye on everything going on around him.

Those who knew Henry Teague best conceived a lasting affection for him. They knew that he liked people and that he wanted them to like him. Never married, and having nobody closely related to him, he turned naturally to

IN THE MIDDLE of July 1877 the Cog Railway conveyed to the summit a printing press and the whole outfit for a daily newspaper. Henry M. Burt of Springfield, Massachusetts, was responsible for this. He conceived the idea on one of his earlier visits to the railway.

It is quite remarkable to think that on this mountain peak there was a railway, a hotel, a telegraph, and a newspaper. This was the beginning of the printing of *Among the Clouds,* which appeared in two daily editions for a third of a century. Printing was set up in the old stone Tip-Top House. Mr. Burt continued for twenty-two summers as editor and publisher of this paper until his death in 1899.

The "devil's shingles," or "slide boards," were used to send a special edition down the mountain at a mile a minute. But most of the time the devil's shingles were used by the track inspectors for sliding down the mountain. The all-time record run on one of these devil's shingles was two minutes and forty-three seconds, made by Patrick Camden many years ago. A customary slide down was ten minutes. They were used by track inspectors up to about 1930.

his railroad, and his hotels and his college boys as his "family." Henry Teague, known as "The Colonel" to everybody on the railroad from Mike Boyce, the oldest engineer in point of age and service, to the rawest college boy, was a great believer in profit-sharing. The bonuses that he distributed at the end of nearly every season helped many a student pay his next year's college expenses.

Many colleges and universities have been represented by student workers on the Mount Washington Railway. Dartmouth and several southern colleges have been most often in evidence. 100 boys more or less were hired each summer.

Among Henry Teague's early improvements was the development of Marshfield at the foot to the railway. Here he built modern cabins, as well as a large and commodious log cabin restaurant and souvenir store. This attractive log structure was erected in 1939 following the damage caused at the Old Base Station by the hurricane of 1938. In its center is a huge stone chimney with two great fireplaces, said to be the largest in New England. There is seldom an evening when a fire is not needed.

An important element in Henry Teague's success was his selection of an assistant and successor in the person of Arthur S. Teague, for several years vice president and general manager, and after Henry's death in 1951, president and superintendent of the railway. The two Teagues met in the fall of 1931, when Arthur was a senior at Clemson College in South Carolina, and Henry, on his way to Florida, was visiting colleges to recruit next summer's crew.

Arthur started work in 1933 after graduating in engineering, and a bond of friendship developed which became a firm basis of successful management. Arthur entered the University of South Carolina the following fall to take his master's degree, continuing his summer work with the railway until called into war service in 1941 as first lieutenant of infantry.

Reopening the Railway

It was impossible for me to return to Mount Washington with Art because our third daughter, Frances Stratton Teague, was only one month old. She was a small baby and needed expert medical treatment for several birthmarks, which had to be removed as two of them were cancerous. Accordingly, Art took me and the children to Philadelphia where I was to spend the summer with Mother while Dr. Pillsbury, the well-known dermatologist, removed Fanny's birthmarks with acid injections and dry ice treatments, spaced regularly through the summer.

Art kept me well informed about his activities on the railroad. This letter, written on May 8, gives some idea of how much had to be done before the first passengers could ascend the mountain:

My dear darling,
The day I arrived I looked over the plant and the men we had here. I left the next morning at 5:00 A.M. and drove all over New Hampshire, Vermont, and Massachusetts to see old employees. At St. Johnsbury, Vermont, I saw Allan Fillion, an old engineer, but he can't be at the railway this season. From there I drove right down the Connecticut River, just the way I came up.
I stopped at White River Junction to see some men the Boston and Maine were laying off and I may get some of them. I could use a dozen more laborers and I am offering 85c an hour.
I then drove down to Keene, New Hampshire, where I saw old Mike Boyce, the senior engineer on the railway. Mike came up to the railway in 1919. Well, I talked Mike into coming up and he will arrive tomorrow. I will pay Mike $1.20 an hour.
I then drove to Nashua, New Hampshire, where I saw another engineer and he is not coming up as he has a good year-round job at the International Shoe Co. From Nashua I went to Narick Hardwick Co. in Manchester where we buy lots of material. I wanted 25 kegs of nails (100 pounds to the keg) and they laughed. I got 25 pounds of each size I wanted and was glad to get them.
From here I went on up to Lawrence Whittemore's home, just outside Concord, New Hampshire, where I spent the night. He used to be assistant to Mr. French, president of the Boston & Maine Railway, and is now president of the Federal Reserve Bank of Boston.
I drove on to Pittsfield, New Hampshire, and then came back to spend the night with Whittemore. Mrs. Whittemore said she had not forgotten the fact that we were going to get a wedding present which was long overdue, but she was going to wait until we stopped flying around! They were quite bugs on antiques so I have my ideas.
Darling, I'll stop for to-night and try to continue tomorrow night. I was gone for three days and arrived back here last night. The weather here is freezing every night. We have many snow banks all around the base. Today we have rain and sleet. I am feeling fine and I hope you and our little ones are also.
With all my love,
                                                                "Art"

Marshfield Station in the early 1960s.

Several days later Art mentioned he was working with the crew up on the track and had gotten just over the first hill after the Ammonoosuc River. He also mentioned he had talked with the general foreman of the Boston & Maine roundhouse and with the car superintendent. He expected to get one man to work up on the Cog and a boilermaker and helper to test the engine boilers. Each spring the boilers are hydrotested, usually under 148 pounds of pressure, before the Cog Railway opens for the season.

Art made a point of stopping at the state capital office building where he spent a part of an afternoon visiting with Mr. Everett, state road commissioner, and Mr. Johnson, the chief engineer of state roads. They mentioned that the state was expecting to spend between $42,000 and $50,000 building 1-7/8 miles of new road to the base. It would start at Fabyans Station and go straight some distance away from the Mount Washington Hotel. It would then come out at the first opening about three quarters of a mile behind the hotel where it would join the old road. About half would be completed soon, but the highway department was having difficulty getting labor.

Art always visited the Public Utility Commission* which oversees the operation of the railway, inspecting both the track and the equipment. All this is done routinely each year, and it is very important to know the people with whom one has to deal while operating the railway.

Art was enjoying his work, although he mentioned that Uncle Henry got in his hair every now and then. Henry had become diabetic and some days was difficult, mostly impatient because he didn't feel well. Coal strikes and then strikes on the railroads which shipped coal to the Cog Railway worried Uncle Henry, and Art wrote that there was enough coal on hand for only limited runs until the end of July.

Somehow Art managed to get things done on time, including replacement of ties and other essential parts of the three and a quarter miles of track. Busy as he was, Art managed to go down and talk to the Littleton Rotary Club.

Rounding up employees was the number one problem. Six of the old engineers agreed to return, and gradually all of the other categories of workers were filled. Mr. and Mrs. Charles Raymond were hired to start pricing and arranging the souvenirs in the gift shop which they would run. At the same time Mr. and Mrs. Gardner Campbell agreed to operate the Summit House at the other end of the track, 6,293 feet above sea level. Now that it was the end of May, Art reported that the trackwork was completed three quarters of the way up the mountain and all was going well. Each morning he boarded a special train with the track crew and worked with them for ten hours, stopping only to eat lunch from a dinner pail like the rest of the gang.

May was followed by the usual June blackflies, after which the little no-see-um bugs appear. While the children and I were sweltering in the city, Art was swatting bugs and sleeping under two and three blankets. Warmer weather followed, enough coal arrived, the summer operation went smoothly, and I was soon counting the days for the railroad to close and release my husband to his family once more.

Life at the Base

Following 1947 our life settled into a routine, commuting to Philadelphia to spend the winter months there and back to New Hampshire for the summer and fall. The Cog Railway season ran from Memorial Day until October 12, Columbus Day.

* At one time the commission was called the Public Service Commission.

Harold Adams (left) and William Livingston turning a shaft in the shop in August, 1965.

When driving toward the railway on the Base Road, the first building one passes on the left is my home, a chalet-type building, from which I can look up the mountain and observe most of the railway's operation. The original structure was Uncle Henry's home, and (as I shall relate later) it burned in 1965 and was rebuilt. In back of the chalet on the left is the boardinghouse constructed in the 1800s and used as the men's dorm. Leading from the enginehouse is a string of eight cottages for married employees.

The railway track starts in front of the enginehouse where the locomotives are stored and maintenance is performed. The next building is the car shed used to house the coaches, and beyond is the girls' dorm. Farther up the track on the right are the ticket office, an attractive log structure; Marshfield House, in which are the gift shop, cafeteria, and railway offices; and the passenger loading platform.

At first I found it difficult to adjust to living conditions at the base. In the spring the winds howled and the rains poured down. During the fall the winds howled very much more, and the rain turned to sleet and snow because we were at 2,700 feet elevation. By the end of October everyone was glad to go down the Base Road back to the comforts of civilization, except Jimmy, the caretaker, who remained behind, snug in the old boardinghouse with the warmth of the big coal stove in his kitchen. A former trapper, Jimmy loved the winters at the base and seemed to hibernate there like the bears and other wild animals which were his friends.

For me there was one danger I feared then and still do—lightning. We had some of the severest lightning storms I have ever known. This was partly because the railroad track acted somewhat as a lightning rod, the balls of fire riding down the entire length of the steel rails like a train. Some of the men reported wild experiences when caught in storms on the mountainside. Jitney Lewis had a hole burned right through the steel toe of one boot!

One time I saw a ball of lightning run the length of the flagpole to the ground, then dig a trench clear out to the Base Road. Hiding my fear from the children wasn't easy, but I forced myself to remain calm and apparently indifferent during even the worst storm.

Another problem over which we had no control was the behavior of our personnel. Very much like the weather, some employees were often temperamental, changeable, and unpredictable. Regardless of who might be sick, fail to appear for work, or create an unexpected problem, the trains had to run on schedule, and this often took its toll on Art—as well as on the entire family.

I soon adjusted to these changes, however, and learned to enjoy our life at the base. Mount Washington is like a magnet. Once you

I HAVE SEEN many girls and boys come and go. I have found that working here at the railway has helped many of these young people to mature quickly because each must accept responsibility, and those who cannot do this are asked to leave at the end of their first year.

I love to see our men return and ask for work on the railroad. It isn't because the pay is good but because they have interesting and unusual experiences and comradeship with their fellow employees. This railway is unique, we all love to be in its "one big family," and it teaches each one of us to give and take.

The "Ammonoosuc" in front of the engine shop.

have lived there, you want to come back again and again. Part of its charm was the people, both the employees, many of whom returned year after year and most of whom caused no difficulties, and the men and women of the North Country who became my people and my life. Those many years spent at the base in the White Mountains made my life there a rich experience.

Family Growth

Art and I continued to be blessed with new additions to our family. During our first summer at Mount Washington we had Janie, Margie, and Fanny, but in 1949 I deserted the base for Philadelphia in order to have our fourth child born there. Anne Tillman arrived on schedule, on August 15. All went well, and I was soon back with the family and remained there until we closed up in October.

In January of the following year Janie, now six years old, came down with diabetes, remaining in a coma for more than a month at Children's Hospital in Philadelphia. Finally Dr. Wallace Dyer, a

world-renowned diabetic specialist, pulled her out of her coma, reg-
ulating her system with protamin zinc insulin and regular insulin.
She was known as a brittle diabetic and recovered quickly, but her
illness changed all our lives.

Dr. Dyer recommended a definite exercise routine for Janie, and
Art suggested horseback riding. The doctor agreed, and that is how
our family entered into the horse world. Ironically, it was through
necessity to save the life of one child—and later it was to prove the
death of another.

We bought a pony and Janie took riding lessons at Byers Academy
on Rex Avenue. The academy was near the new home Art and I had
built all by ourselves with the help of one laborer. Our plans were
approved at city hall, and we built our two-story home at 201 Rex

ONE TIME when National Newspaper Association members visited the Cog Railway, Art
told them a story which appeared as "Editorial Comments" in *The Union
Leader*.

"Arthur and Ellen Teague entertained the visitors on the Cog Railway on
Mount Washington, and for good measurement staged a reception and buffet
at their Marshfield restaurant. Colonel Teague said he remembered an incident in June 1950 when the editors, after meeting in Providence, journeyed to
the mountains. There were about two hundred in the group, and Colonel
Teague had them board six of his railway cars. Just as the last man stepped
aboard, an agent from the Internal Revenue Service appeared to register an
objection that no federal tax had been collected. The late Ed Ellingwood, state
publicity director, who was on hand, volunteered to file a protest at the
Portsmouth office. Colonel Teague reported he still has, framed, the apologet-
ic letter he received from the collector of internal revenue, who said an error
had been made by the agent, that the tax was due only if a charge had been
made. Since there was no fee, there was no obligation to Uncle Sam. The tax,
the collector explained, is a percentage of the sum charged. Inasmuch as the
charge was 'nothing' the percentage of 'nothing' was 'nothing,' the collector
concluded. His audience laughed heartily as Colonel Teague related the
story."

Avenue from the foundation up. We obtained the hardwood pine flooring from Vermont and likewise all the cedar for the closets —giving it a touch of our beloved New England.

It was a good location, affording us opportunity to hitch the pony to our sleigh and take the children for long rides. The house proved a popular attraction to all of the family, including Uncle Henry, who would stop for a night or two en route to Florida.

Uncle Henry's Death

It was October 4, 1951, just ten days before we were to close the operation. I was in our house at the base when Art came in and sank into a chair. I knew immediately that something had happened, but I could never have guessed the truth.

"Ellen," Art muttered without looking up, "Uncle Henry's gone; he just died."

"Died?" I repeated, incredulous. "Uncle Henry's dead?"

Somehow it seemed impossible to think of that big hulk of a man dead—gone—no longer overseeing the operation that spanned the side of New England's highest mountain. I glanced up at Mount Washington and could see a train making its way down the summit while another waited for it at Waumbek junction. Trains were still running—the railroad would continue to operate, but who would own it? And more important, who would manage it? Within minutes our world had collapsed.

The next few days were a blur to all of us, but we managed to keep our schedules right up through the closing day, and then we learned the railroad's fate. As mentioned in an earlier chapter, in gratitude for what his alma mater, Dartmouth College, had done for him back in 1938 when it advanced the money needed to repair the hurricane damage, Uncle Henry had left the entire railroad property to the college. Furthermore, because Uncle Henry never was able to manage his money, the railway was required to pay $10,000 annually for ten years to the college in order to satisfy certain bequests which Henry had also stipulated in his will.

With the end of the "Colonel Henry Teague era" Dartmouth College became the railway's new owner, and at the request of President John Dickey and Treasurer John Meck, Arthur Teague remained as its general manager.

Engines No. 6 and No. 9 at the Waumbek switch.

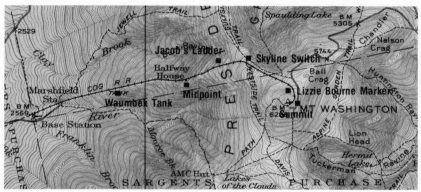

*L*ADIES AND GENTLEMEN," the conductor announced from the front of the coach as the train jolted to a stop, "we will make a short stop here at Waumbek Tank while the crew performs a couple of chores."

Every year the crew of the last train down has responsibility for draining the Waumbek Tank and then disconnecting all pipes which might still hold any water. While the men were busy preparing the wooden tank for winter, the passengers left the coach, welcoming the opportunity to stretch and take their last look at the magnificent mountain scenery.

Waumbek—the name of an early Indian tribe—flashed through my mind as I stood on the narrow platform waiting for the men to finish their job. Waumbek. Why did it have some special meaning to me, an association I could not quite grasp? Then I remembered. It recalled an unusual conversation Art had with Philip Hamberg, a well-known reporter from New

81

York City who loved the mountains and the railway. The setting for this delightful conversation took place on the back porch of the Mount Washington Hotel in Bretton Woods. Art and Phil each sat in an old rocking chair and rocked in silence for a few minutes as they enjoyed the grandeur of the White Mountains.

Art finally said, "Isn't it beautiful? I never stop thinking how beautiful it is around here. Isn't this a fine place to watch a railway?" Phil said that it certainly was.

As Art talked, he kept an eye on the mountain and spoke of the origins of the railway, which I have related.

"You know, when Old Peppersass was retired in the 1880s, she did quite a bit of traveling around the country. She was exhibited at the Columbian Exposition in Chicago, in 1893; stayed eleven years at the Field Museum in that city; moved on to the Louisiana Purchase Exposition in St. Louis, in 1904; and was then bought by the Baltimore & Ohio Railroad. In 1927 the B. & O. brought her out for its 'Iron Horse' fair held in Maryland. In 1929, the engine, then sixty-three years old, was shipped back to the Base Station of the Cog Railway which was then owned by the Boston & Maine." Phil listened eagerly.

"On July twentieth, the six New England governors held a celebration, and Old Peppersass was scheduled to climb up the mountain once again. Several hundred guests were invited—Jack Frost, the engineer, had five passengers aboard. The engine moved up without difficulty. The plan was to stop at the top of Jacob's Ladder, but when they got there it was decided to keep going. Just half a mile above Skyline it was decided to back down. Old Peppersass performed beautifully for half a mile on the return journey. Then, suddenly, a tooth broke off the cogwheel, and Old Peppersass jumped up. When she came down, she was off the tracks, roaring down the ties. Jack Frost hollered 'Jump' so all jumped except a photographer who went back to get his camera. A moment later Old Peppersass took off from the ties at a curve and the photographer fell off and was shattered on the rocks. The engine came to a stop below Jacob's Ladder. Miraculously, her boiler had not exploded, but she had made her last trip, and high time, too. She was repaired, and I have placed Old Peppersass on permanent exhibit at the Base Station."

Art was still looking at the mountain. "Train just going over the horizon," he said. "I can't keep my eyes off the hill. We grossed about $145,000 last year, but our expenses are high. Road maintenance is $30,000 for tracks and trestle and so on. We spend $30,000 or $40,000 for maintenance of locomotives. We just bought a new boiler for $10,000. Then, there

82

is $25,000 for labor and $20,000 for coal, and $10,000 for insurance, and $10,000 in real estate taxes. We're tided over by the Souvenir Shop. Look at her chugging up there now! That wisp of smoke means a great deal to me." Art pointed to another tiny speck, headed up cog by cog. "Oh, there are a lot of things I'd like to do. I'd like to have the summit proclaimed a National Forest. But mostly I want to keep going, smoking away like a steam engine!" Art pointed to the plume of smoke.

"Number 4 is at Waumbek," he said with a glance at his watch, "and right on the button, too!"

How proud Art was of the railway! I learned to share it too.

"All aboard, all aboard for the Base Station," the conductor cried, and in no time the passengers were back in the welcome warmth of the waiting coach. The doors were closed, and we started off on the last leg of our trip—the final part of my Cog Railway experience, which would mark a turning point in my career. Again I thought back over the years, and it was inevitable that those three dear ones I had lost should come to mind as I was about to end this chapter of my life. Art, as I said before, seemed very close to me on this journey, and now I was aware of Lucy too . . . and Janie . . .

6

Triumph and Tragedy

OUR FIFTH DAUGHTER, Lucy Simpson Teague, was born on April 16, 1953, and was delivered by Dr. John Montgomery at the Jefferson Hospital, as all my babies had been. A big strapping infant, she was easy to care for, and I left the city early in June to join Art at the base. We took the pony with us in a trailer, and I can remember the birthday party we had for Anne that August when she turned four. She looked like a natural rider and promised to be a good equestrian in our horsey family.

The year 1954 was remembered for two interesting events. The first was a special "snow train" Art operated in May for the Nashua Ski Club. The skiing in Tuckerman's Ravine on the east side of the mountain often lasted until mid-July, and whenever requested, Art quickly prepared a special ski train, loaded the passengers in the coach and their skis in the tender, and sent them aloft to the summit. That same year the Reverend Hollis Hastings of Lisbon officiated at one of the rare marriages on the East's highest peak. Nancy Schott of Des Moines, Iowa, and Bruce Monsette of Lisbon, New Hampshire, both employed at the Mount Washington Hotel, were joined in marriage. A few days before their wedding winds had gusted up to one hundred miles an hour, but on their special day the breeze clocked at fifteen miles an hour and the temperature a cool forty-two degrees, it being the end of August.

An important event occurred in 1955 which brought great benefit to the tristate area of Maine, New Hampshire, and Vermont. John W. Guider, president of the Mount Washington TV and an Annapolis Naval Academy graduate, erected a transmitting station at the sum-

84

mit. It was believed to be one of the strongest stations at the time, operating on a frequency of 180 to 186 megacycles, with its coverage extending as far into Canada as Quebec City and Montreal, and west to Buffalo, New York. The studios of WMTW were located in Poland Spring, Maine, and the station was later purchased by Jack Parr.

The most important event for the Teague family during that same year was the appearance of Charles Arthur Teague, our only living son, who was born on February 24. Again the Jefferson Hospital played host to mother and infant son with Dr. Montgomery attending. Now that we had a boy at last, Art and I agreed that our family of five daughters and one son was complete!

In August 1955 Art, our friend Cass White, and I drove over to Guildhall, Vermont, to look at a farm which had 110 acres, including 10 bordering the Connecticut River. The owner, whose father had died recently, was anxious to sell, and we returned that day with a written agreement to purchase the property. It seemed like an ideal weekend retreat while the children were growing up.

For the next twelve years Carroll Reed ran the farm for us, raising corn, vegetables, hay, and oats, and maintaining a herd of a dozen or so cows. As the children went away to school and married they no longer wanted to use the farm, so I sold it in July 1973.

ON ONE TRIP after Dartmouth College had acquired the railway, President John S. Dickey and other Dartmouth College officials were on board for a ride to the summit; they had hardly been gone five minutes when the train jolted to a stop. Art jumped from the coach and ran back to the locomotive. In a minute he returned.

"The train will proceed," he announced, "as soon as the fireman recovers his shovel."

The fireman happened to be a Dartmouth boy, who reported that the vibration had shaken his coal shovel from the engine and that it had fallen into the bushes under the railway's wooden trestle. The train didn't start until he'd recovered it.

The skiers embark on Memorial Day, 1954.

Mount Washington Weather

Sharing the summit with the TV building and the hotel was the
U.S. Weather Bureau's observatory, one of the most important in the
country. It was here that the record wind velocity of 231 miles per hour
was recorded; little wonder that weather fans throughout the country
always are interested in knowing what the conditions are on Mount
Washington. Winter winds often average 100 to 185 miles an hour.
When Charles was four, I took him with me on the train to the
summit, and just as we stepped away from the coach and headed for
the Tip Top House, a mighty gust of wind blew Charles straight out.
Fortunately, I had hold of his hand or he might have landed in
Tuckerman's Ravine. The men at the observatory keep the railroad
posted on weather conditions at the summit, and when the wind
becomes too gusty, trains are canceled for safety's sake.

While I am mentioning the wind, let me say that a seventy-minute trip on our steam trains could be quite an experience. The wind was sometimes so strong that it blew the coal off the fireman's shovel, and occasionally the vibration would shake the shovel off the train. One of our engineer's glasses blew off, and Mike Boyce's teeth rattled out. Now and then the backdraft of the firebox from the boiler singed the hair and eyebrows of the firemen. On a dry day the hot sparks frequently set fire to the grass beside the track. When that happened, the next down or up train would have to stop and extinguish the flames. It could be an exciting trip!

The Modernization Controversy

At one point *New Hampshire Profiles* ran a poll asking its readers to decide whether or not the Cog Railway was out of date and should be replaced with a monorail. A comparatively few unsentimental people wanted to get to the top faster than the Cog engines could travel, but the great majority of our Granite Staters have loved the Cog for its

I T WAS HARD to keep the cost of everything down, but by working with his men Art was able to inspire their cooperation and much was accomplished. In his early years with the railway Art installed a Pelton Water Wheel driven by the force of water coming down the mountainside from the Franklin Brook through a six-inch pipe. This waterwheel ran a generator which produced electric current. One half of the power turned a water pump, which delivered thirty-eight gallons a minute to the Summit House tank through a two-inch pipe, and the remaining current provided lights for our base colony as well as electric power to run the machinery in the base machine shop. This saved many extra thousands of dollars, since we used DC current, and not AC.

Improvements were made on the size of the axles—new six-inch-diameter axles. Art also used hard and tough steel, the same specifications used in airplane crankshafts. He redesigned the cog gears of cast steel with extra teeth for added safety for the public. There were just so many reasons to be grateful to Art for all he did for the railway. In the machine shop every imaginable part could be made and precision work done.

The observatory in the solid grip of winter in an earlier day.

uniqueness and wanted no change. This sentiment was further borne out by the pros and cons we had regarding the coaches.

The question arose as to whether we should build more wooden passenger cars or aluminum-and-steel coaches which would be longer, carry more passengers, have larger windows for viewing, and be easier to keep clean. Many passengers had registered complaints about cinders flying into the wooden coaches when windows were open and the wind blew the wrong way.

Accordingly, work began on redoing the old coaches at the base to make them safer for the passengers. Art changed wooden chassis to steel chassis and inserted ball bearings to make rolling easier, but he made sure to retain the old original appearances both outside and inside where possible. These procedures were carefully carried out on all the wooden coaches.

Numbers 3 and 4, the old Laconia coaches built by the Laconia Car Company in Laconia, New Hampshire, were the first done. These had been built about 1875. Two of the old coaches (Numbers 1 and 2) have been taken down to the original paint design, so when you come to the Cog Railway and see the bright yellow coaches with the red trim which look like circus cars, you will know this is what they looked like one hundred years ago. This explains why we are an operating museum.

In 1955 Art and I approached the Budd Company to see what new coaches would cost. When Art learned that the company would charge $55,000 for a single aluminum-and-steel car, Art decided to build one himself. The next three summers, he, Ed Chumley, and my nephew, David Morgan, worked on the aluminum coach, constructing it for $19,000. To celebrate its inauguration in regular service, we invited Governor Lane Dwinell to christen it. He and his nephew, John Newman, rode the new car to the summit and spent the night at the Summit House. Although many people enjoyed riding in the new coach, the majority preferred using the old wooden coaches because, I believe, they were seeking nostalgia.

It was this same nostalgia which made the overnight trips to the summit so popular. In 1958 a round trip cost $4.60, and we offered a package deal for those who wanted also to spend the night at the Tip Top House. Supper was served on tables covered with red-checked tablecloths with a candle on each, and sometimes an employee would provide dinner music on the old upright piano. I remember lying in bed and experiencing the howling of the ever gusting wind, the rattling of the wooden shutters, and the delicious shivering under several blankets. Then everyone rose early in time to view the glorious sunrise. People talked freely with each other and left in the morning feeling that they had had an experience they would never duplicate anywhere else.

Murder on the Cog

The State Employment Office sent Gilbert H. Gonyer, forty-five, of Lancaster, New Hampshire, to work for us during the 1959 season. They told us nothing about his past record, that he had been released from the Maine state prison three weeks previously after serving a term for theft, or that he had done time in Connecticut and New Hampshire for forgery.

One Sunday in July I had set out for church and stopped at the camp where the Bretton Woods Boys Choir lived when a woman came running up to me.

Edward Chumley, Governor Lane Dwinell, and Art Teague at the dedication of the Chumley coach in 1958.

"My husband's just been murdered—down there on the road," she gasped, out of breath and terrified. "Oh, it's terrible, the man shot him in cold blood! Help me, please!"

I tried to comfort and calm her. "Tell me what happened so I can help," I said, and after she had gained control of herself she told me what had happened.

She was Mrs. Eli Gendron of North Woodstock and had stopped with her husband on the Base Road for a picnic. Shortly thereafter Gonyer, whom the Gendrons knew slightly, came along and asked to share their food. When they had finished their early lunch, he took out a revolver and forced them to drive him down Clinton Road to the old railroad crossing. Without warning he shot Mr. Gendron, then turned to his wife and said: "You'd better get going, or you'll get the same thing."

When she finished telling me her story, I called the state police and then drove to where she said her husband had been murdered. The man was slumped in the driver's seat as his wife had said, and there was no heartbeat. After the police arrived and I told my story, I returned home, inasmuch as the search for the killer had already started. Later we ransacked every closet, dresser, bed, and corner of the boardinghouse at the base and finally found a bloody shirt rolled up in a closet. The murderer was caught, confessed that robbery had been his motive, and received a double life sentence.

This unfortunate event took much of the pleasure out of that summer season. Nevertheless, everyone's spirits perked up somewhat in September when the Cog Railway played host to a number of famous botanists who stayed at the summit for three days to study the alpine vegetation which draws many scientists to the Mount Washington alpine garden.

The Railroad Is Ours!

"Ellen! It's ours at last!" Art ran into the room waving a letter as he came toward me. Then he leaned down and gave me a big kiss.

"You mean the Cog?" I asked, hardly daring to believe that it could be true.

"Yes, my dear!" he said with emphasis. "It's back in the Teague name, only this time it will be a team ownership and management." We walked over to the window together and looked up at the mountain. Art put his arm about me, and for a couple of minutes we just stood there, watching the trails of smoke where the engines were hard at work.

"It's hard to believe," I murmured, thinking of how eager Art had been to own the railroad someday and wondering if it would ever come to pass. Suddenly, as I watched the plumes of smoke rise and then drift with the wind, I felt that something within me had expanded out beyond my body and up the mountainside to its very top to blend with our beloved mountain and make me a part of it. Now, this minute, not only the railroad but a portion of the Presidentials was ours, even though it was only the narrow strip on which the track was laid. We were not just property owners, but hereafter we would share in both the joys and the responsibilities of maintaining and preserving a bit of our nation's heritage.

Thus, our years with the railroad immediately took on new meaning and importance. Humbled as I stood there, I thought of the magnitude of what we owned, but most of all I experienced tremendous pride in Art because it was he who had made this happen.

"Let's tell the children." Art broke our silence. "After all, they're part of this business, too."

Somehow the actual process of closing our purchase on November 20, 1962, seemed trivial after that first thrill of learning that the Cog was ours. We made a down payment, and the college gave us a mortgage for the balance of the purchase price, the mortgage being paid off finally in February 1981. The sale included the railroad and its rolling stock of seven steam locomotives and eight passenger coaches; the thirty-six acres at the Base Station; the Marshfield House with its gift shop, restaurant, and kitchen; and the surrounding cabins. Dartmouth College retained ownership of its summit property.

Thus Art and I began our journey of ownership, our three oldest girls working in the office, gift shop, and restaurant of Marshfield House during the summer months. Jane was now nineteen, Margie sixteen, and Fanny fifteen. As each of the children grew older, they contributed more and more time and effort to the business. It was fun for all of us to be working together; and the girls were paid salaries and bought their own school clothes.

Horses, Horses, Horses

Life was not all work on the railroad by any means. Our principal outside interest was attending the many horse shows which were held in the area. This became a family activity, as we joined the New Hampshire Horse and Trail Association and then began participating in many events. Gradually we accumulated good show horses, including Morgans, thoroughbreds, and the pony. The girls were proud of their mounts and kept them immaculate. We always attended Essie Serafini's Sugar Hill Horse Show which featured a lavish buffet supper for the participants. For many years Enzo Serafini was our commentator at North Country shows, and he also served as president of the New Hampshire Historical Society.

I used to enjoy driving my horse, Polly, in the nearby Lancaster Fair. We all rode in the family classes; Margie and Anne were our hunter seats; Janie, Fanny, and Lucy entered the equitation saddle seat and pleasure-riding classes in the shows. We had a large cogwheel painted on the back of the horse trailer with the phrase: "Pleasure Horses Riding in Pleasure." Naturally, we advertised the railway as we met people at these shows.

Over the years we attended shows in New Hampshire, Massachusetts, and Pennsylvania, winning many trophies, ribbons, and championship ribbons. At the New York Madison Square Garden, Janie and Margie came in second in the Morgan pair class. One time Fannie's horse almost rode over a judge as she froze in the saddle, but fortunately the horse just missed him. Janie, who was responsible for our horse fever, adored her Morgan horse, had beautiful form, and won many championships. This therapy apparently worked and kept her diabetes under control. As for Anne and Margie, they were our hunter seats and did well in those classes, while little Lucy loved her horse, Black Magic, who accompanied her wherever she went. Little Lucy . . .

As the years rolled by we purchased more horses, at one time owning ten, and we even went in for breeding thoroughbreds, having several fillies and colts in the stable at one time. Art bought a second-hand yellow truck at a Vermont auction, and this enabled us to carry a number of the horses along with the trailer whenever we attended shows. Thus, we relaxed and played as a family, always enjoying our togetherness.

The children kept busy working and playing during the summers, but their education and urban social life were not neglected during the other months. Janie attended my alma mater, the Agnes Irwin School, then took two years at the University of New Hampshire, finally transferring to Drexel University in Philadelphia. Margie and Fanny attended public school, went on to Franconia College in New Hampshire, and finished at Eastern Baptist College in Pennsylvania. Anne chose Stevens, a private school, then attended Eastern. Fanny and Anne each earned two degrees in teaching, and then both taught school.

All the girls had their debutante parties and attended the Assembly Ball except Anne, who chose to marry instead of coming out. Lucy, approaching her teens, was a beautiful tall girl, her gracious manners making her popular and beloved by almost everyone. Little Charles was the musical child, playing his trumpet and taking lessons from Elvira Murdock, a member of Ina Ray Hutton's "All Girl" Orchestra. Charles went to Penn Charter School for two years and then transferred to Chestnut Hill Academy, going to boarding school in Stony Brook, Long Island, starting with the eighth grade. After several summers at boys camps and a trip to Mexico with his schoolteacher, he joined the rest of us at the Base Station.

Tragedy on the Base Road

As late as 1963 our road into the base consisted of four miles with twenty-two pronounced winding curves and about one mile of fairly straight highway connecting U.S. Route 302 to the base of Mount Washington on its west side. Each year Art and I tried to keep track of how much money had accumulated from special funds provided by the National Forest Service for service roads. I would then write the governor and tell him the amount of money which should be available for repairs to the road into our base.

I had been concerned for some time over the condition of the road with its many treacherous curves. On many occasions I drew on my nursing skills to attend injured motorists who were involved in accidents. In one mishap a doctor's car overturned; fortunately, he was not killed, although he was seriously injured. Again and again we would remind the governor about this dangerous condition, but nothing was done about it until after the fatal accident.

"Mrs. Teague?" the trembling voice asked over the telephone.

"Yes?"

"Been a terrible accident on the Base Road down by the big boulder. Can you come right away?"

I grabbed my "little black bag" with some emergency first-aid items and drove my black station wagon as fast as I dared to the site of the accident. Because of a huge rock the road bent sharply to the left and over the years many drivers had sped toward it too fast to negotiate the curve, but until today no one had been killed.

Someone helped me lift the lovely young girl out of the wreckage and place her on the blanket in my car. I did what I could to ease her pain and then drove to the Lancaster Hospital twenty-five miles to the west. Nine days later she died in the Mary Hitchcock Memorial Hospital in Hanover, New Hampshire.

Why, Art and I asked each other, why do we have to wait for death before we correct bad road conditions or put up traffic lights at dangerous intersections? I immediately wrote Governor King who came up to inspect the road personally. Shortly thereafter he sent me the following letter:

Dear Mrs. Teague:
Enclosed please find a copy of a memorandum from Highway Commissioner John O. Morton with regard to plans for correcting the dangerous situation of the Base Road that serves the railroad Base Station.
Corrective work will start immediately following the closing of the October 12th weekend.
If you have any further suggestions or if you notice that the work is not proceeding as scheduled, kindly get in touch with me.
Sincerely,
John W. King

The text of Highway Commissioner Morton's memorandum read
as follows:

Dear Governor:

At the time of my visit with you on Friday, September 20, you mentioned a
fatal accident involving a young girl in the vicinity of the railroad base
station at the foot of Mt. Washington.

On checking this location with my people I find that they are most familiar
with the accident and its location. The road is what is known as the Base
Road serving the Base Station. This is a highway that has been constructed
and reconstructed out of special funds that come to my department from the
U.S. Forest Service and which we utilize to build service roads contained
within the White Mountain National Forest area. The fund is a small one
and generally has to accumulate two or three years before a worthwhile
project can be undertaken.

The section where the accident occurred is on a curve and is contained
within the project that is programmed for reconstruction. Because the
railroad generally operates until the weekend of October 12 it is customary
for us to delay construction until the railroad has stopped operation for the
summer season. Construction will remove the boulder that caused the fatal
accident and do much to improve the general alignment and grade of this
particular section of highway.

Your calling this matter to my attention is appreciated.

Sincerely,

John O. Morton, Commissioner

Before we closed the Cog Railway that same season it had become
apparent that several of the state politicians were eager to purchase
the summit of Mount Washington. Finally on March 30, 1964, the state
agreed to buy the land and buildings from Dartmouth College, which
still owned the property. The sale precipitated a minor crisis for us.

The Trial Balloon That Burst

Shortly after the state acquired the summit, Russ Tobey, the commissioner of the Department of Recreation and Economic Development, began to feel his oats. He suggested that the Cog Railway track
should be relocated and run only two thirds of the way up the mountain, ending its trackage in the vicinity of Skyline siding.

Art and I were dumbfounded! Nothing could be more detrimental to the continued success of the road than cutting off its access to the summit. If this were to happen, we agreed that we might as well close down the operation entirely and let the state suffer the consequences in its loss of tourist business.

Fortunately, Tobey's proposal quickly became front-page news throughout New Hampshire, and soon Governor King was receiving letters of protest. Here is one such letter, which was typical of the many which were pouring into the State House.

Dear Gov. King:

Ever since the state acquired title to the summit of Mt. Washington I have been increasingly concerned with the long range plans for this historic and famous piece of property. Some items in the press of late indicate that Mr. Tobey is anxious to change things on the summit to such an extent that the summit would become little more than unoccupied land with a view, a view available only on clear days.

I think it is important that things remain pretty much as they are for in my opinion Mt. Washington without the Tip Top House, the hotel, the TV and weather stations, and the parking lot and cog railway terminal would indeed be just another pile of rocks similar to many such mountains of greater and lesser stature in this country. Tourists are persuaded to visit Mt. Washington for two reasons: the means of getting to the top and the attractions at the top once they get there. Many go in spite of the weather because the scenery is not the primary reason for their going.

The main attraction at Mt. Washington without doubt is the cog railway. It has been this way for almost a century but increasingly more so in the last

THREE PRESIDENTS of the United States have ridden the railway. Ulysses S. Grant during his term of office was aboard with his wife and son, Jesse, on August 27, 1869. Sylvester Marsh welcomed President Grant. Then Rutherford B. Hayes and his wife and two sons rode the Cog Railway on August 20, 1877, and President Franklin Pierce also rode the Cog one summer.

decade. It is unique in all the world and I think that sometimes we here in New Hampshire are so close to this major attraction that we discount the tremendous appeal it has to others all over the country and the world . . .

I too sent a strong letter to Governor King and received the following reply:

Dear Mrs. Teague:
Thank you for your kind letter and the enclosures, which I found very interesting.
I rather suspect that Russ Tobey's observances regarding the relocation of the Cog Railway were in the nature of a trial balloon. While I ordinarily have a great deal of respect for his thinking, I can assure you that this particular idea found no sympathy with me at all.
From the general reaction throughout the state, I would say that the balloon was quickly punctured and fell to earth.
The Cog Railway is one of our major attractions in New Hampshire, and its many friends would not tolerate interference in its operation.
Sincerely,
John W. King

We won the fight, but Mr. Tobey was to have his revenge the following year when Art and I leased the Summit House from the state. The commissioner proved difficult to deal with, demanding that we make so many improvements to the property that it became hard to make a profit. We had to hire more than thirty employees before we could institute a package deal of riding the Cog and spending the night on the summit. Although we began to draw crowds, we seriously questioned whether it was worth the extra work and aggravation. Had we known then what the Summit House would eventually do to the Teague family, we most certainly would never have leased it.

Some Notes About the Teagues

What was happening to the eight Teagues during these years? Art retired from the U.S. Army Reserves in 1963. A veteran of thirty-one years in active and reserve duty, he received numerous certificates of appreciation and was honored by a retirement dinner at the Philadelphia Naval Base officers club.

About this same time we built a second house which was not as compact as our first on Rex Avenue. This was more spread out with its large living and dining rooms, library, six bedrooms, and two and a half baths. We had two acres just beyond the city line near good schools and shopping facilities.

In the spring of 1965 Margie announced that she wanted to join a group of her college classmates who were going abroad. When I talked it over with Art, he said that the only way to finance the trip would be for me to sell some of my stock, which was not worth much then. I wanted Margie to have the chance to travel because I had never had the opportunity and believed it would be very beneficial to her. When Fanny learned that Margie actually might be going, she felt badly because the girls were very close and had always shared their pleasures—but how could I send both girls?

I called my broker and explained the situation. At the time I had shares of Air Products, which was then traded over the counter.

THE PEOPLE who live in the southern part of New Hampshire have a great deal to learn about the hardships experienced in the north. Not only are the winters much more severe in the North Country, but most of our business here depends on tourists. It is important that the legislature and governor realize this and provide adequate funds for advertising the state's tourist attractions.

From time to time Art and I invited the governor and his council to hold their meetings at the top of Mount Washington. This gave us a chance to ride the railroad with them and enabled all of us to become better acquainted. Governor Wesley Powell was one of our favorites. Following a council meeting at the summit, he wrote:

"I just want you to know how delighted Beverly and I are with the beautiful leather photograph album containing the souvenir pictures of the governor and council meeting on top of Mount Washington. You certainly were most thoughtful and kind to send us such an attractive memento of a most enjoyable occasion.

We shall look forward to visiting with you some time this summer and meanwhile send to you our warm wishes."

"Wait a bit and let me get back to you," Teddy Freed counseled, after I told him that I was hoping to use the proceeds of the sale for the girls' European trip. Before this came up, I had planned on using the money for their coming out party and the Assembly Ball next fall.

I really said my prayers, asking that if possible Fanny be permitted to share the experience too. My entreaties were answered when several weeks later the telephone rang. It was Teddy.

"Ellen," he exclaimed, "you're rich!"

"What do you mean? What happened?"

"Your stock has gone way up," he said. "You've made several thousands."

The girls not only had their trip from June to September, but they had their dresses to be worn at the Assembly made for them in Paris. In addition, making the girls more attractive then ever, Fanny had a French haircut and Margie a French wave in her hair!

While the sisters were visiting the Mediterranean islands, Athens, Paris, and England, Janie was working at the base as our cashier and Anne was waiting on customers in the gift shop. Charlie Teague occupied himself making slingshots and putting garter snakes around his neck to frighten the girls in the dorm. He was also taking trumpet lessons and climbing the Ammonoosuc Trail by himself. Always a rascal, but a cute one at that, I once caught him standing on the big rock outside the gift shop proudly "peeing" to the amusement of some people and disgust of others. Meanwhile, Lucy was always with her horse, Black Magic, or feeding her calf in the horse barn. She loved animals and considered them her best friends.

After the season closed, Art and I took three of our employees with us to Montreal for two days and nights of fun and relaxation at the Queen Elizabeth Hotel. Horse shows and night clubs gave us a much-needed break before our return to the base where Art worked with the other men to close up the operation. Before they had finished, Art and I decided to make a quick trip to Philadelphia to check on the children and the house, leaving the shop crew and caretaker to complete their chores during the first week in November.

Then early in the morning of November first our phone rang.

I shall never forget Art's face as he held the receiver, listening intently and unable to talk.

"All right, we'll start right out," he muttered, "be there as quick as we can."

He replaced the phone and stared at me speechless.

Remains of the Hut after the fire of 1965.

"What is it?" I could not imagine what had happened from his end of the brief conversation.

"They've been fighting a fire at our home since five o'clock—it's all gone—everything." He covered his face with his hands, and then we tried to comfort each other.

We rushed back that day, but there was nothing we could do. We had no insurance on the house, and we had lost everything we owned there, including priceless patterns for machinery, memorabilia pertaining to the railroad, trophies won at horse shows, everything.

"If the chimney withstands the winter," Art told me, "I'll build you another on the same site."

Our friend, Florence Morey, who ran the Inn Unique down in Notchland (Hart's Location), wrote to the *Laconia Evening Citizen* about the fire. The following article appeared in the next issue:

*From former Rep. Florence Morey of Hart's Location we learned of the loss
by fire of the home of Colonel and Mrs. Arthur Teague at the base of Mount
Washington. The large log home with its yellow trim near the Base Station
of the Cog Railway was leveled in the early hours of November first.*

*Colonel and Mrs. Teague had been collecting historical material for the
centennial of the Mount Washington Cog Railway. These were carefully
stored in the large house at the Base. The home called "The Hut" contained
much in the way of old time cog railway items, too, cleverly put to useful
purposes by Ellen Teague. All these along with clothing and horse-show
trophies won by the Teagues' daughters were lost.*

*"It would completely floor most people," Mrs. Morey said, "but you know
the Teagues and their spirit."*

*We express our sympathy to the Teagues and agree with Mrs. Morey on
that spirit of the Teagues and their Cog Railway.*

We received heartwarming letters of sympathy from friends far
and near. Here is what former Governor Hugh Gregg said:

Dear Arthur:

*It wasn't until I read yesterday's paper that I knew of your terrible fire loss
at the Base Station. Had I known sooner I would have contacted you
immediately to offer any assistance possible. But, be that as it may,
certainly if there is anything at all which we can do in the way of lining up
or assisting in the procurement of doors, sash, blinds, cabinets or anything
along those lines, you know you have only to yell.*

We stand ready and willing and hope we can be helpful.

Best.

Sincerely,

Hugh

When we returned to the base in the spring of 1966, we found the
chimney still standing, and Art immediately went to work, planning
the construction and consulting with Fred Pilott of Whitefield. That
summer the girls used the small cottages near the engine shop while
Art and I kept Lucy and Charles with us down in what I called "The
Hen House"—*Old Peppersass's* old shed. We lived in organized chaos

and somehow got through the season. Business was good and I thanked God for our blessings.

Our Trip Abroad

In the spring of 1967 Art and I decided to celebrate our twenty-fifth wedding anniversary with Marion and Gib Holt, two of our closest friends, who also were observing their quarter century of marriage. We met and made plans to take a trip to Spain. Art knew that I had always wanted to see the Alhambra, and it was planned we would arrive there on April 23, my birthday. I had never been abroad and loved the idea of going to Spain to see its bullfights, architecture, churches with their beautiful stained-glass windows, and the famous graves. I never thought I would see any of this, and now it was about to come true.

We flew to Madrid and spent two weeks in Spain. Then we took the ferry across the Mediterranean to Tangier. Here I visited my first cave, saw where the Mediterranean meets the Atlantic Ocean, enjoyed Spanish Morocco, and traveled through parts of northern Africa where Franco hid his troops. To me it was like walking back into biblical times.

In Paris we lived it up doing the usual Folies-Bergère and night clubs, visiting Notre-Dame Cathedral, the Eiffel Tower, the Louvre, and the Left Bank. Of course we lunched at the sidewalk cafés and purchased wonderful perfume. From there it was London and then home to Philadelphia. Art left immediately for New Hampshire to get the railroad operation under way. Tom Baker went with Art, driving the yellow truck, and I waited for the children to finish school before following.

Problems with Mr. Tobey and the State Again

Opening the Summit House was never easy, but this year it was more difficult than ever. Ice had accumulated around the furnace, and Art had to chisel it away before he could get the ancient monster going again. The old Summit House had been built in 1915. It was a strong building, constructed to withstand the terrible winds, but the all-important heating plant was antiquated and the state made no effort to improve it.

As Art and his men worked to open the hotel, the state workmen who were supposed to help with much of the work slacked on the job.

Even the state engineer quit when the weather wasn't what he thought it should be. As a result, Art and his crew were often doing work that was the state's responsibility while Tobey's men were sitting in the Summit House by the warm fireplace.

Mr. Tobey was completely unsympathetic to Art's problems, it being his position that as leaseholder the railroad was responsible for repairs and other maintenance. His attitude was reenforced by the Senate Finance Committee and the Attorney General's Office, which ruled that repairs were no responsibility of the state.

Art and I rejected this ruling completely. We had worked for years to cement good relationships with the state. Our package deal —which was dependent on the use of the Summit House—had attracted many new visitors to us and helped the state's tourist business generally. We felt that the men in Concord had a responsibility not only to us but also to the citizens to maintain properly what they had purchased and to keep it in good condition until they were ready to undertake new construction.

The final blow struck when we received notice that the Department of Health and Safety had decided we could not use the Summit House for overnight guests until we undertook and completed extensive renovations. I cannot describe Art's reaction to this news. Our national advertising—featuring the overnight trips—had all been placed; our employees had been hired to operate the hotel; and all our train schedules had been planned with this business in mind. Things between us and the state went from bad to worse. In the end we were permitted to open only the lunch counter, the souvenir stand, and the toilets.

Art was very hurt and discouraged. It was a blow to his pride and to his pocketbook as well. An article in *The Union Leader* reflected the sentiments of many people who were unhappy at what had happened.

The Summit House

Addressed to William Loeb: The controversy over the future of the Summit House on Mt. Washington greeted me as I returned this month from Catholic University in Washington. I was greatly disappointed to learn that the hotel will be closed this summer, thus depriving many visitors of the experience of spending a night on New England's highest peak. It's not just the idea of spending a night on the mountain, it's the whole atmosphere of the Summit House at night on the mountain.

The Summit.

I had my first taste of this last summer when I went up with a friend from Philadelphia. As neither of us had ever camped out before, we decided it might be best to spend our first night on the mountain in the hotel. (The second, we spent at the Lakes-of-the-Clouds Hut.) It was a truly great experience. A fine dinner to start the evening—entertainment furnished by a visiting choir—the absolute blackness of the night outside knitting the guests into such friendly company—the warm courteous service of the employees and the simple feeling of welcome in the old rooms—all these contributed to an unforgettable experience, no less than frosty gales outside. It would be a real tragedy if the old Summit House were closed.

August 4, 1967

Things did not improve over the summer; in fact, everything seemed to go from bad to worse. Art became sick, and I took him to the Mary Hitchcock Memorial Hospital in Hanover, New Hampshire, where he was under the care of Dr. Milne. He had symptoms of angina but after a week was dismissed and returned to the base. He was now taking several medications but seemed to get progressively weaker and was unable to cope with the demands of the railroad and his heavy work schedule. He tried to the best of his ability to keep things going, but it was increasingly difficult for him to concentrate and complete what he hoped to accomplish.

On August 4 our lawyer, Jack Middleton, and our accountant, Tony Poltrack, came to the base for a directors meeting. Art attended but disagreed with so many of their decisions that the meeting was adjourned. Art then returned to our yellow cabin for a nap, whereupon Jack and Tony asked if I would ride over with them to Guildhall, Vermont, to our farm to get some vegetables.

I asked Art if he would mind.

"Go, by all means," he said, "I'll be all right."

We weren't gone more than two hours, and when I drove up front of Marshfield House, Jitney Lewis came running up crying: "The Colonel—the Colonel has just shot himself."

We drove immediately to the yellow cabin.

"He's in the bathroom," Jitney managed to tell me, and I forced myself to go there where I found his body slumped on the floor. I put my hand on his still warm back but I knew he was gone.

Today I could not describe how I felt then, even if I could remember. As a nurse I had met death many times but never before with someone so near and dear. Probably my first instinct, thanks to my medical training, was to take charge, see what had to be done, and do it. I must have sensed a need to be with my children, comfort them, and give them such understanding as I could. My own shock and grief, deep as they were, nevertheless were lessened temporarily by my immediate perception of what had to be done—by me. The enormity of our loss was not grasped yet. Rather, it was as though I were dealing with an emergency which called for quick decisive action with no time for tears.

Tom Baker and Bud Nye cleaned up the bathroom for me—it wasn't easy because they too loved Art. I forced myself to stay in the cabin doing all I could to help the children through the next difficult hours. It was little Lucy who found her father, having gone to the bathroom and at first thinking that someone had placed a dummy on the floor. She then went into shock, and I kept her with me for several days thereafter. She could not even cry, but the day of the funeral she finally broke down and this released her pent-up emotions. Going down the aisle of Saint Paul's Church in Lancaster, New Hampshire, she put her head on my shoulder, making it harder for me to carry on—but I was grateful that the tears had come at last.

Charles was just twelve years old and at first quite uncertain as to what had happened. Janie, on the other hand, with her diabetes, had an immediate blood sugar rise. Anne was just numb, she was so attached to her father. Fanny and Margie supported me the best they could, but none of us understood—not even I.

The church was packed for the funeral, which was conducted by Hobart Heistand, the rector. Both the day and the service were beautiful, and I was greatly comforted by the many friends who came to be with us, even the governor being represented. A large American flag covered Art's casket, and he was buried in the Railway Cemetery up on the hill overlooking Lancaster.

After the interment someone slipped me an envelope, and while driving home I opened it to find that it was from John Meck, Dartmouth College treasurer, stating that he would help me with the railroad in any way he could. I can never be grateful enough for that expression of sympathy and assistance.

The following articles appeared in *The Union Leader:*

Col. Teague at the time of his death was recuperating from a heart attack suffered shortly after his return to Mt. Washington in early June from his home in Philadelphia.

Upon his return to the mountain he was confronted by the news that State Departments of Health and Safety had ruled that the Summit House, famous hostelry on the top of Mt. Washington, required extensive renovation, pending which it could no longer be operated as an overnight hostelry. Col. Teague had never been notified of the state's findings, although they had been made many months earlier. He had operated the hotel on lease from the state and had as usual geared his nationwide advertising program to the assumption that passengers on the Cog Railway might, as in past years, enjoy overnight accommodations on the mountain.

Teague also found that gale winds had blown down a water tower which supplied the summit facilities, as he had predicted to state officials might happen if the state-owned structure were not made more secure.

GOVERNOR AND COUNCIL
TO THE RESCUE OF MT. WASHINGTON

But too late, it appears, to allay the concern of Colonel Arthur S. Teague, Cog Railway president and "most decorated" World War II soldier.

Edward Cullen [of the Governor's Council] said that the lack of a commissioner has placed an "unfair burden" upon the shoulders of every

division head in the department in making them responsible far beyond the
normal scope of their duties.
"It was the place of a commissioner to see to it that a realistic program for
the entire summit was instituted as soon as possible after the state acquired
it in 1964, and to then appear personally before not only the legislature but
even the 1965 session and back the program to the hilt. I'm sure something
could have been started even back then to prevent this present emergency
from developing."

And so it went. I listened to the politicians' excuses and tried to cooperate with them. We continued to operate the Summit House after Art's death, but just as they had said back in the spring, it was only food, souvenirs, and toilets, hardly much stimulation for advertising New Hampshire and Mount Washington.

We held a meeting of the railway board of directors at the Base Station; I was named president and Jitney Lewis manager. I took Art's place on the board, the other directors being Mike Haney, Jack Middleton, and Tony Poltrack. Having been so closely associated with Art in the operation of the railway and all its facilities, I felt that I could state with honesty and conviction that "I would carry on just as my husband would have wished me to do."

Meanwhile, every mail brought a stack of condolence letters from far and wide. There were letters from many of the captains and lieutenants who served under Art; letters from prominent New Hampshiremen such as B. J. McQuaid, Frank A. Tredinnick, Jr., John W. King, James C. Cleveland, Sherman Adams, Stanton Becker, Edward M. Brooks, Don Tibbetts, Dr. Charles Everett Koop, Leonard A. Stevens, attorney Jack B. Middleton; and many, many more, to say nothing of old friends, business acquaintances, and others who knew and loved my husband. I especially treasured one note written by an officer who had served under Art. One sentence read: "Those of us who knew him under the conditions of battle had unbounded respect for his courage, ability, and dignity as a man."

In memory of Art, Essie Serafini and some of the people involved with the horse shows got together and arranged to purchase a large silver punch bowl on which the winners of the special Teague class would be inscribed every year, each winner receiving an engraved replica of the punch bowl.

So much for this sad period of our lives.

Exactly two weeks after the day Art left us, Anne and Lucy decided that they would carry on with the horse show they had planned to attend in Keene, New Hampshire. They had both ridden there the previous year and enjoyed entering the various classes.

"Mother, is it all right if we go this year?" Anne asked. The girls obviously needed a change and something to take their minds off what had happened, but in looking back now, I wonder why I ever let them go. Anne had had a very busy day at the railway working in the gift shop, and Norman Koop did a full day's work on the trains. As for Lucy, she had been working steadily on Black Magic to get him ready for the show.

By the time we finished supper it was dark, and they still had to load the two horses in the trailer. Lucy came to me and asked if she should go, evidently not feeling entirely sure that she should leave me.

"Go, by all means," I told her. "You must get your points to win the pleasure horse class at the fall banquet."

"Thanks, Mom." She gave me a hug and a kiss. "Be careful, please." I can still feel her little arms around my neck. Later Fanny told me that Lucy went down to her and asked her to take care of me. Fanny has never gotten over that. She loved Lucy so very much.

Meanwhile I went to see the group off. There were Lucy, Anne, Cindy who was Lucy's friend, and Norman Koop who had agreed to drive them. He used the station wagon with the hitch on the back because our yellow truck, which we usually drove, would not start.

Feeling very lonely I went to bed in our yellow cabin. Sometime around midnight I heard a noise, looked out on the porch by my bed, and saw Lieutenant Genest, the state trooper based at Twin Mountain Barracks—Troop F. My heart stopped beating for a second or two, and then I rushed to the door.

"I have some bad news," he said. And I knew.

"Is anyone dead?" I asked.

"Yes."

"How many?"

"One."

I was afraid to ask, but I finally did.

"Who?"

"Your daughter Lucy, she was killed on Route 93, just before the exit to Tilton, Bridge 52.

I closed my eyes for a moment, unable to believe what he said. It was Art all over again. Then in a daze I put on my clothes, walked over to the Lewises' cottage, and knocked as gently as I could. Barbara Lewis came to the door, and I told her there had been an accident, that Cindy was alive but Lucy was dead.

At first she seemed unable to comprehend what I had told her. Then she placed her hand on my shoulder.

"Jitney and I will drive down to the hospital," Barbara said gently. "Trooper Genest can take you over to the undertakers."

My friend and pastor, Hobart Heistand, was at the door to meet me, and inside I found my sister Marnie and her husband, Jack Morgan, who had come to support me. I identified Lucy, felt her cold stiff body, and just could not accept it. It was too much—she was such a sweet, lovely girl, the best, and here she too was gone. Hobart said a prayer for me as we stood by Lucy, and then I turned and left for the hospital.

Anne told me the story later, but it is too sad to recount it all now. She was driving. Somehow the car went off the interstate, rolled over, and Lucy was pinned beneath the car. Once more I learned how hard it is to live with tragedy, but somehow God gave me the strength and faith to carry on. I knew that I was here for his purpose, to help others, and I prayed that he might help me the rest of my days.

Lucy was buried in the cemetery beside her father. "She dwelt unknown, but few could know, when Lucy ceased to be."

"But she is in her grave and oh, the difference to me."

Bernie McQuaid wrote the following tribute in his newspaper, *The Union Leader:*

Just what is one to say of this, seemingly heartless manifestion of the will of an inscrutable providence? Fate, it would appear, selects for its cruelest shafts only the most vulnerable targets.

None more so than the gentle Ellen Teague, famed always for the motherly sweetness and affection which she lavished not only upon her own brood but upon the boys and girls who come every year, from many parts of the country, to work and earn money for their education, on the Cog Railway.

It is this maternal solicitude, backed by the Almighty's aid, on which her

The author and Jack Middleton head for the disaster area on September 17, 1967.

friends must now prayerfully rely to see her through her troubles. Mean-
while they may rightfully call upon the entire state to assist her in every
way possible in the continued operation of the railroad, a responsibility she
bravely assumed following the death of her husband.

–B. J. McQ.

How grateful I was to Bernie, and how humble I felt. I was beginning to wonder whether or not I could make it through the season, for
I was almost ready to collapse. Somehow I summoned up reserve
strength and courage—I had to do this for the children's sake, and for
Art's railroad too—and I carried on.

September 17, 1967

Time marched on and it was fall, foliage was turning, and the
weather was holding well, but my spirits were not with the sunny lazy
days of that fall. Sunday, September 17, was a beautiful day and
business was good. We had all worked hard; everything had operated
like clockwork on schedule; and there was just one more train to come
down the mountain. I remember that it was about half past five when
the phone rang.

"Can you come to the ticket office immediately?" the voice at the other end asked.

"Yes, but why?"

"Something's gone wrong up at Skyline switch."

"What? What is it?" I demanded to know.

"Coach is derailed—also the engine."

I couldn't believe what I was hearing. We had never had an accident like this all the time we had operated the railway. What could possibly have gone wrong?

"What else?" I asked.

"Some passengers have been injured—and there are some deaths."

I replaced the receiver and looked up at the mountain. Mount Washington can be a great source of inspiration and strength, but now I felt a sense of horror in contemplating it.

Art had reminded me again and again that in case of an accident, the first thing I should do was to call the Public Utility Commission, then our lawyers, then the police, and finally the ambulance and hospitals. But we had no phone at the base, only plant phones on the railroad. I knew there was nothing for me to do but dash down the Base Road to Fabyans—six miles away—and use the pay phone at the station.

As I ran over to the ticket office I planned what I had to do. First, I told our employees there to pull out the work car which had a flat bed, and while that was being done others should round up all the blankets they could find around the base. I designated two employees to go up on the work car to do whatever was necessary while I drove to Fabyans. Fortunately, I was able to put through the calls, and the police came quickly to block off the Base Road so that only the ambulances could come through.

All this I did in a daze. Once again my nurse's training gave me the ability to plan and keep myself from panicking. I dashed back to the base and found that the train had departed and that all my instructions had been carried out.

Up on the mountain the most seriously injured were loaded onto the flatcar and immediately on reaching the base were transferred to the waiting ambulances. I asked the drivers to go directly to the Littleton Hospital, the area's largest. The police had already notified other hospitals about the accident, and it was arranged that critically injured passengers would be checked out of the Littleton Hospital by

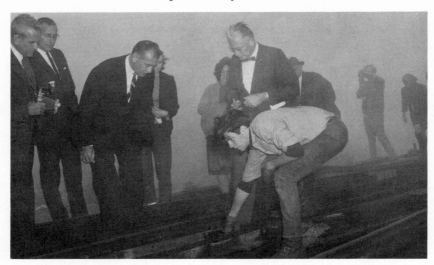

Members of the Public Utilities Commission inspect the faulty track.

the doctors there and sent to the Mary Hitchcock Memorial Hospital in Hanover, which had the most extensive medical facilities in the North Country. The less severely injured would be sent to Berlin, Lancaster, and St. Johnsbury hospitals.

A siren announced the arrival of the North Conway emergency first-aid truck. About the same time someone turned on emergency floodlights, and as if by magic, stretchers, oxygen, medication, and bandages were on hand.

Sometime in the early evening Governor John King and former Governor Lane Dwinell arrived to give me the strength that took me through that terrible night. Next morning the governor ordered "a full scale investigation" by the state's Public Utility Commission.

The accident was caused by a human error. Bob Kent, who usually took the first train up the mountain, told Governor King that he would often find our Skyline switch thrown. This switch is located where the Appalachian Mountain Trail crosses under the Cog Railway track. We had reason to think that an occasional hiker threw our switches, and I suspected that this was what had caused the accident—but how could it be proved?

No trains ran the next day, and the Public Utility Commission sent

Public Utilities Commission members prepare their statement to the press.

word that it was going to close us for the rest of the season. Then I remembered what Art told me:

"Ellen, always keep the trains running." This I tried to do.

There were some expressions of sympathy, but most surprising —and gratifying—was President Lyndon Johnson's message of sympathy for the victims of the accident and offers of aid should any assistance be needed.

Two weeks later I was invited to speak to the Littleton Rotary Club at the Thayer Hotel. We had a bus tour from Georgia which had just arrived there, and it was scheduled to go to the summit the following day. In addition to the Rotarians, the people in the tour, the Governor's Council, and the Public Utility commissioners were in the audience. George McAvoy encouraged me to speak to them frankly about what had happened and why there would not be a reoccurrence of that tragedy. I gave a long talk and felt that it was helpful to have the members of the tour listen too.

The next morning the tour bus drove up to the Base Station. When I saw it coming, all I could think of was: "Ellen, keep the trains running."

Meanwhile, the Public Utility Commission was meeting in the

Looking toward the Summit from Waumbek.

dining room where a representative of the Associated Press was also present. A public-address system had been set up so that the commission's decision could be announced to the crowd at the base.

"Ellen, you can't do this," my friend and attorney, Jack Middleton, counseled as he glanced at the tour bus. "Tell them you can't run the trains."

"Ellen, keep the trains running!"

Swallowing hard, I left him and walked into the dining room. When the men saw me they stopped talking. I could feel the tenseness in that room but I took a deep breath.

"I am waiting to load a tour," I announced. "These people have driven all the way from Georgia and wish to ride the trains." Then I left and paced up and down in front of the building.

The Lord was with me again. A few minutes later the announcement came over the loudspeakers: "The Mount Washington Cog Railway is now running and will operate the rest of this season. The Commission has found that a human error was responsible for . . ."

I cannot say more about this terrible thing, but I cry whenever I think of it and the deaths of little ones on the train that night.

I do know, though, that some good came out of that tragedy. At the time Dr. Harry McDade was having trouble trying to get the Littleton Hospital to adopt his plan for meeting emergencies. That night of the accident he was able to apply his idea. It was so simple and so effective! One doctor would call four physicians, each of those four in turn would call four, and so it went—and it worked. Perhaps God has his plans and we are here to carry them out.

Business picked up immediately as passengers filled five trains waiting to ascend Mount Washington, by the Cog, to the summit. No matter what happens, it seems as though life is like the streams. We keep moving along, and we move along not knowing what we will run into. That is the way I felt then. I just kept going. Actually, I doubt that I could have made it through the balance of the season without the support of Red and Charlie Lovett who own Lovett's Inn-by-Lafayette Brook in Franconia, New Hampshire. Charlie told me that "The Lord never gave anybody problems which they couldn't handle." This gave me reassurance and courage.

The end of the season came. It was the last day, and I could hardly talk, I was so tired. I said my goodbyes and then collapsed on my cot in the yellow cabin.

The ambulance came. I could hardly get my breath. Dr. Harry

McDade gave me an intravenous injection of morphine directly into my vein to stop the pain. After three tragedies, I had finally caved in, and I remained in the hospital two weeks. Then Janie and Margie drove me back to Philadelphia.

This was how I ended my twenty years with Art at the Cog Railway.

Building the track with "Old Peppersass," about 1867.

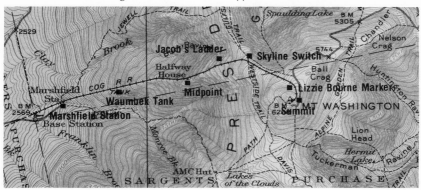

"B ASE STATION, LAST STOP! Watch your step getting off,"
the conductor called as the train glided to a gentle stop. It was
getting dark, and the passengers quickly left the coach to rush
to their cars and get on their way.

Ellen Teague was the last to step from the car. The act of passing
from the coach to the wooden platform marked her final separation from
the railroad, both symbolically and actually. As she did so she asked herself
if this had really been the very last trip she would ever take on her railroad.
Doubt, then panic seemed to paralyze her. Had she acted too hastily? Alone
on the platform, she stared at the engine, a thousand memories and questions revolving through her mind.

It wasn't easy to walk away from a business which had been a good
part of your life for thirty-two years, which had claimed your husband,
which had taken you through the depths of grief and tragedy with an

117

accident and then elevated you joyously as you celebrated its one hundredth birthday. The Cog had been responsible for her meeting Art in the first place; then it had captured her and, at one time or another, each of the children too. The satisfaction and pride that came from knowing your "baby" had carried hundreds of thousands of men, women, and children safely up to the summit and back again could not be brushed aside casually. Once you were a "Cogger," it was hard to be anything else!

She did not have to sell the railroad and thereby banish it from the Teague name, an ownership which had run and loved it for so many years. Wasn't she the chairman?

The engineer tooted the whistle and started toward the enginehouse. She became aware of the smell of soft coal. The nostalgic aroma recalled the life and activity she had lived and loved through most of her married life. It seemed to be calling, saying, "Don't go, Ellen, don't forsake me."

No, she did not have to sell the road even though right now four buyers wanted to acquire it. Perhaps her decision to sell had been unwise. Sixty-eight was not old. Look at Colonel Sanders, who started his Kentucky Fried Chicken when he was ten years her senior!

Still, for each argument against selling there was an equally persuasive reason to turn her back on the whole operation and never return. There were problems every season—no business operates without them—and certainly not a railroad like this! Then there was the matter of her health. She had suffered a heart condition when Janie was threatened with a toe amputation, and wisdom dictated retiring now. Heavens! She was already three years beyond normal retirement age! With Art gone and the children no longer there to help her, she had to admit that the fun and sense of family togetherness were gone. What was more important, selling the road would assure her financial independence for as long as she lived. She would be free to do many of the things she had always dreamed of . . . travel . . . build a little home of her own up here in the North Country . . . help the children when they needed her . . . visit the grandchildren . . .

"Ellen," Faith called, "can you come to the office? Time to lock up."

"Be right there," she replied, and as she walked slowly toward the building she wondered what she should do and could not but think back to August 1967 when she became president after Art's death. Busy years they had been—maybe her first decision was the right one—on the other hand, perhaps she had been too hasty . . .

7

Madam President and Chairman

AFTER RESTING for a month in my Philadelphia home, I returned to "thinking" because Margie and Tom Baker wanted to get married—and soon! After several family consultations we agreed to ask Hobart Heistand to marry them on December 23 in Saint Paul's Church in Concord, New Hampshire. I decided to give them a honeymoon in Nassau while the rest of the family spent the Christmas holidays on our Guildhall, Vermont, farm.

The 4:30 P.M. ceremony took place as planned, and a reception followed at the nearby New Hampshire Highway Hotel. Janie was Margie's maid of honor. The bridesmaids included Fanny and Anne; their cousin, Becky Morgan; and a friend, Katherine French of Philadelphia. Tom's niece Brenda Baker, was the flower girl.

A number of our Philadelphia friends flew up for the wedding. All our Cog employees were invited, and a number of them attended. I shall long remember that day. It was the first bit of happiness the family had experienced together during that tragic year. When Margie and Tom were saying goodbye, they hugged and kissed me gratefully.

Planning for the Centennial

January 1968 arrived too quickly, for I knew that it meant I would have to face a number of important decisions, the foremost being the choice of a manager for the railway. Jitney Lewis did not want to return, which left me with two candidates: Bruce Sloat and Lionel M. Rodgers, a friend of Art's. Before I interviewed them I knew that I would like to have Lionel in the post because of his personality, honesty, and sincerity. Lionel accepted my offer and in so doing

119

agreed with me that the most important task facing us was planning the railway's centennial celebration the following year.

Lionel's wife, Margaret, was eager to work with Janie and me on the planning, as was Ida, Lionel's mother. In addition, I appointed a working committee which included Mrs. John Guider, Mrs. John Meck (the wife of the Dartmouth treasurer), Mrs. George Carter, Mrs. Jack Middleton (who served as treasurer of the centennial), and Mrs. Anthony Poltrack. We worked hard all during the year, and with such loyal and enthusiastic helpers, I looked forward greatly to the event.

The first item on the agenda was contacting Charles Penrose, president of the Newcomen Society. Art had expected to speak with Mr. Penrose about the possibility of addressing the society in connection with the anniversary. I wrote Charles Penrose and received a prompt reply saying that he would like me to speak to the society during 1969. He also asked me to become a member, and I accepted, although with some trepidation, not having done anything like this before.

In taking on this responsibility I realized that I would have to do considerable research for my speech, and although it was time-consuming it proved a lot of fun. The big job, though, would be planning for two dinners: one on July 3 to mark the date when *Old Peppersass* first made it to the summit of Mount Washington, and the second on September 19 when the Newcomen Society would meet.

E MILE ROULEAU, our unique Belgian, who is now buried in Colebrook, could speak French but not read. I enjoyed reading his letters to him in French. I can't remember a day when Rouleau wasn't here. He built our fires each morning in the Marshfield House; he saw to the trash; and he chopped down so many trees for wood and for building. He helped at whatever job was asked of him and was everyone's friend, but he had two bad habits. He drank and he loved his women. Before coming to work for the Cog, Rouleau had been a woodsman and could do the work of ten men. He helped build the Marshfield House in 1938. How can one ever forget Rouleau?

I chose the Crawford House for our July celebration and decided to ask a number of dignitaries and make it an outstanding occasion. Nothing, I decided, must change this date, and the entire affair must be perfect from start to finish. I formed a committee, and each of us was assigned various tasks. At this point the most important jobs were for some of us to write invitations while others sold advertising space for our centennial booklet. Our planning progressed well during all of 1968.

Meanwhile, I represented New Hampshire at the first National Conference on Tourism and the Energy Crisis. The delegates approved a ten-point resolution which called for reaffirmation "that freedom of travel is a fundamental freedom" and stressed tourism's significant contribution to employment and national expenditure. I had opportunity to talk at length with John Lombard, an Amtrak executive, about the possibility of train service being extended to the White Mountain area, but, alas, it never materialized.

Prior to opening our 1968 season I announced that the Cog Railway would allow up to 50 percent reduction in fares to foreign visitors. The resultant publicity was well worth the discount, although we actually carried few such passengers.

Our employees worked hard in the best interest of our passengers, and Lionel kept his watchful eye on the little steam trains. He was a railroad buff, and that was reflected in the way he made certain that the cars were swept, the windows washed, and the exterior of the coaches kept clean too. During the season I felt free to leave the railroad in Lionel's charge as I accepted invitations to speak before various organizations—valuable preparation for the year to come.

When we closed on Columbus Day the books showed that business had been off somewhat from previous years, but that was to be expected because of the accident. I was satisfied nevertheless, since it is a characteristic of transportation that following an accident traffic declines, then gradually regains its former volume. Now and then someone would ask about the accident, and when we explained that it was due to a human error, they invariably accepted it and sympathized with us.

Our employees had been eager to put up a memorial plaque for Art on the big boulder near the restaurant, and I had hoped this could be done before 1969. My wish was gratified, for the boys donated the necessary money, and Joe McQuaid wrote the following poem to be inscribed on the metal plate:

He worked so damned hard
It tears me apart,
He gave us his love
And he gave us his heart.

I loved him as a father,
He was one to me.
If I have to have a hero
Let it be he.

The water runs swiftly,
It hurries to the open sea.
It wants to be lonely,
It wants to be free.

I think of the Colonel
And then I think of the sea,
And my heart is happy,
Because he is finally free.

The fire grows dim now,
The stars begin to shine,
The embers that are dying
Smell fragrant as my wine.

This poem must end now,
There is no more to say,
The fire has died down
The embers blew away.

The trees stand so tall now
They touch the silent sky.
I look at that mountain
And ask myself why?

Why is he gone, God?
Why did you take him away?
Couldn't he have lived
For just one more day?

If this life is precious
And you hold it so dear,
Why is he gone, God?
Why is he not here?

He loved this mountain
And he loved its life.
He worshipped his children
And he loved his wife.

Another Wedding and a Sad Problem

"Mother, Norm and I want to get married," was Anne's greeting when I returned to Philadelphia in November. I wasn't quite prepared for this.

"But what about college?" I asked. "Don't you think you should complete your education first? Why waste what you've already put into it?"

I knew there was no way of dissuading the young people from what they wanted to do, so I talked with my good friends, Dr. and Mrs. Koop. They indicated that they would see Norman through the rest of his college education if I would do the same for Anne. What could I do but accept the proposition? Thus, Fanny, Janie, and I got together to arrange for another marriage.

Anne was married on December 27 at Saint Martin-in-the-Fields in Chestnut Hill, Pennsylvania. We held the reception at our home, and the Koops gave the young couple their honeymoon. I was very happy for them and especially pleased that they could return to college.

Now for a note of sadness in the midst of the fun of planning for the wedding. Just before the happy event Janie discovered a bad infection on a left toe, and when she went to the hospital the doctors decided that it must be removed. This upset me terribly because I did not expect she would lose the toe, and when the doctors told me that after Anne's wedding Janie would have to return to the hospital and possibly have her leg amputated, I had a minor heart attack and was put in the cardiac section. Both Janie and I were released in time for the wedding, but Janie had to use a wheelchair.

Anne and Norm left for their honeymoon, and the night before Janie was scheduled to return to the hospital for the amputation I called Dr. Koop.

"Could you come right over and look at Janie's leg?" I asked. "The infection has spread up to her knee."

He entered the house silently, and I think I was just as quiet as I followed him upstairs. He stood by Janie's bed and watched as I undid the bandages covering her left foot. Janie, who had started losing her eyesight in 1968, turned and stared at Dr. Koop as he examined the leg. I do not know how well she could see his reaction, but he turned to her and smiled slightly.

"Janie, I have seen worse," he said. Then he looked at me. "Ellen, do you want to work?"

"Yes, what can I do?"

He immediately removed his coat and rolled up his sleeves.

"Prepare her foot and sterilize my scalpel in alcohol and get a basin," he directed. I did what he asked, and he then took the scalpel and opened up her entire left foot as she lay there on the bed.

"All right," he said as he studied the foot, "now I want you to run water in the tub and put her foot right under the running water. Do this several times a day."

I looked at him and smiled, as did Janie. We both felt such relief that he had substituted this simple treatment for the drastic operation.

"I'll be back," he continued, "and bring some oxidized cod-liver oil from Children's Hospital." Then I knew that there was a chance of saving Janie's leg. "I'll tell the other doctors what we're doing," he promised as he pulled down his sleeves, "and I'll cancel the operation."

During the next five months I worked faithfully applying the oxidized cod-liver oil and keeping the wrappings on the leg as he had shown me. We saved Janie's leg, but meanwhile she was rapidly losing her eyesight. To keep her from being too depressed I did all I could do to cheer her up and took her to the top eye specialists. They examined, x-rayed, questioned, and talked among themselves but gave us no hope. Fortunately, we had the centennial plans to work on, and this kept her mind busy. Janie was an excellent planner, an intelligent young person, and a great help to me—but the cruel diabetes had caught up with her.

By spring Janie was much better, and her leg was healing so well that by the first part of June she was able to discard the wheelchair and walk independently. On June 14 she and I headed for Mount Washington where she would work as usual as cashier in Marshfield

House, assisted by an employee as needed. She had taken home economics at Drexel and was a great help to me in designing the costumes for our employees who worked in Marshfield House that year.

The Centennial Success

Thanks to our excellent working committee, all our plans for July 3 had been made and carried out with unusual efficiency. I honestly don't think the committee members forgot a thing or overlooked a single detail in their planning, which made it both easy and enjoyable for me. The governor issued a special proclamation:

STATE OF NEW HAMPSHIRE
By His Excellency
WALTER PETERSON, GOVERNOR

A PROCLAMATION

MT. WASHINGTON COG RAILWAY DAY

WHEREAS, July 3, 1969, will mark the exact centennial anniversary of the opening of the Mt. Washington Cog Railway, the first mountain climbing cog railway in the world, and

WHEREAS, Mt. Washington is the highest elevation in our State and in northeastern North America, and its conquest by rail marked an extraordinary achievement by 19th century technology, and an accomplishment which has been copied by engineers in other mountainous portions of the world, and

WHEREAS, its construction was the result of the technical skills and personal traits of distinguished sons of New Hampshire like Sylvester Marsh, Herrick Aiken, and others, whose aspirations and dreams came to reality in the Mt. Washington Railway, and

WHEREAS, in the century since its operations began, the Mt. Washington Railway has attracted hundreds of thousands of visitors to our State, including Presidents of the United States beginning with the eighteenth, U.S. Grant, as well as many eminent men and women from abroad,

NOW, THEREFORE, I, WALTER PETERSON, Governor of the State of New Hampshire, do hereby proclaim Thursday, July 3, 1969, as Mt. Washington Cog Railway Day and I commend this historic anniversary to the attention of the public media of information. I urge that our people everywhere give thought to the history of this enterprise and to the skills of those who built it and who have operated it for the past one hundred years.

At the Centennial dinner on July 3, 1969; (from left) former Governor Sherman Adams, the author, Governor Walter Peterson, and former Governor Hugh Gregg.

As I read the proclamation I could not help but think how difficult it was to reach the base of Mount Washington when *Peppersass* made her first run. The nearest railroad terminated at Littleton, twenty-five miles to the west, and from there people had to travel by stagecoach over primitive dirt roads, a striking contrast to today's highways. That so many visitors would make the long dusty trip into the base was evidence of the new railway's popular appeal.

The day came and everything went like clockwork. The weather was perfect and enabled John Swearingen, Art's cousin and president of Standard Oil of Indiana, his wife, and daughter, to arrive in their own private plane. The other guests of honor gradually appeared and we were waiting for them. Janie and Sally Carter manned the admission desk, giving the guests of honor their special badges and the wives of dignitaries their bouquets. As each guest arrived, he or she was given a table assignment for the banquet.

We had a booth constructed for Ida so that she could sell chances. It was remarkable the way she enticed people to come up and buy. With her pumpkin face and large generous smile, there was no way they could resist her. The chances she sold were for a new Ford George Carter had ordered for us, as well as for other prizes, and a final award, a hundred-dollar bill, for the last drawing. We raised enough money to give $5,000 to the Mount Washington Observatory in memory of Art.

When the guests took their places at the tables, they found as a gift souvenir coffee spoons with a picture of the Cog train on them. Lovely flower arrangements of red, white, and blue had been provided by my dear friends, the Richard Riffs. Mrs. George McAvoy's son, Janie, and I made up the silly names for the menu, which read as follows:

Ball bearing melon, Lake of the Clouds trout, filet mignon a la cinder sauce, timberline potatoes, early bird special peas, Base Station stuffed tomato, Cog track salad, stoker rolls, Centennial parfait, cog wheel cookies, White Mountain mints and Peppersass beverage.

Ivan Task's orchestra from Philadelphia played during dinner, and later the Bretton Woods Boys Choir sang between the speeches—with beloved "Uncle Frank" Hancock conducting.

At the head table we displayed the original patent model on which the entire Cog Railway operation was based, which was conceived by Sylvester Marsh. John Swearingen acted as toastmaster. A Cog Railway alumnus who had worked during the 1930s for four summers, he was a Cogger who lent a very special touch to the evening.

Following the invocation by the Reverend Alexander Hamilton, who later became an executive vice president of the railway, guest speaker, former Governor Sherman Adams, reviewed the colorful history of the railroad and concluded with a poem which is reprinted below. Following his talk, John Meck, vice president and treasurer of Dartmouth College; Alan Smith, president of the Mount Washington Observatory; Lionel Rodgers, vice president and manager of the railway; and I, spoke. The evening concluded with the benediction pronounced by my old friend Hobart Heistand, who said:

Oh God, most holy and mighty, who out of love did create the mountains, land and sea, we pray that Thou wilt grant Thy blessing upon this good land, her people, and her leaders. More particularly we ask that Thou would bless this beautiful state and all those who dwell within her borders. Especially Lord, we pray that Thy continuing love be with Thy faithful servant Ellen and her children; and may the blessing of God Almighty, the Father, Son, and Holy Spirit, be with you and bring you peace and joy in His service. Amen.

The guest list read like a New Hampshire Who's Who: Governor and Mrs. Walter Peterson; former Governors Sherman Adams, Hugh Gregg, Wesley Powell and their wives; Meldrim Thomson, a later governor, and Mrs. Thomson; state senators; other government officials; and Dr. Edward Brooks, Joe Dodge, Warren Noyes—whose father drove the stages through the mountains—and many, many others. The great-grandson of Sylvester Marsh was present with his wife and family, as was a granddaughter, Mrs. Henry C. Short, who brought with her the original patent of the atmospheric brake which her grandfather had invented. (This patent may be seen in the Mount Washington Observatory Museum.) Even Larry Richardson was present—he and Art designed the switches during the 1930s—and several other Coggers, together with my sons-in-law Tom Baker and Norman Koop, completed the crowd.

When the last guests had departed, we drove home and as an anticlimax found that Janie's dog Sassy had just had five puppies all born on her bed. There were four black curly pups and one tan whom we kept and named *Damascus*.

But this was not all! Next morning, July Fourth, Governor Peterson officiated at the christening ceremonies of the new locomotive, the "Col. Arthur S. Teague," which was under construction and on display outside the engine shop. With the governor were Senator Laurier Lamontagne of Berlin and Arthur Tufts, president of the New Hampshire Senate.

Our good friends who edited the *Laconia Evening Citizen* commented that week:

The Centennial observance of the Mount Washington Cog Railway was a tremendous success. Principal credit belongs to Ellen Teague, who has carried on as president of the corporation since the death of her husband, Col. Arthur S. Teague. We were fortunately able to join the group representing the Evening Citizen *at the event, and cannot recall another such elaborate affair more perfectly managed.*

As newspapers are so often required to do, I should like to print a correction to the above statement: "Credit belonged to the entire Committee who planned the event, not to Ellen Teague, and Ellen Teague hereby takes this opportunity to express her appreciation to all who helped make this such an outstanding success."

For an added celebration of the anniversary, all summer we gave every one hundredth passenger a free ride to the summit and back. We also had commemorative coins to sell in the gift shop, and I presented a special Cog Railway trophy replica to a number of horse show classes in memory of my husband.

On important anniversaries like this it is natural to look back and think of all that happened over the intervening years. My involvement with the Cog was for a period which totaled less than a quarter of the railway's lifetime. Much happened during the few years I have recorded here, but the bulk of the Cog's history took place before I arrived at the Base Station. Hence we were grateful for Sherman Adams' poem which sums up the railway's first one hundred years.

THE COG RAILWAY

Now goes it with waumbek mentha NOW,
With the cold and thunderous gale,
The slides that rip her rugged sides,
The blasts her peak assail.

The weather watch, is it still there
Recording the wind and frost
The bleak old buildings grim and bare,
The trails the packers crossed?

The road that scrabbled up chandler's ridge
In tortuous wind and curve
And twisted between steep bank and cliff
That tested the heart and the nerve.

How fares the railroad and the crew
That spirited us into the clouds
With the huff and puff and bituminous smoke
That wrapped us in sooty shrouds.

All's well, old traveller, the mountain's still there
With its shabby old buildings and its frosty thin air
And the carriage road winds in its curling ascent
While the watch keeps its score on the firmament.

Now the railroad is observing the centennial year
Of the huffing and puffing of its custom-made gear
Of the men and the boys whose genius and cunning
Maintained the wood trestles and kept the trains running.

It was Marsh who built it, the first of its kind
From a model by Aiken, but Marsh had the mind
And the courage and fervor to make history take note
Of his great undertaking on a mountain remote.

When Marsh proved his project and gave up the ghost
The Boston and Maine was the reluctant host.
When it lost its hair shirt, in despair and fatigue,
It sold the cog railroad to Henry N. Teague.

Now Teague was a man who was right for his time,
Who had lost all his money and hadn't a dime,
A bullhorn of a voice and confidence galore
Were the tools he employed and he didn't need more.

Impecunious enough for a sound bank to censure
He shook down the railroad and embarked on his venture.
When the hurricane blew down his trestles and track
Dartmouth College came forward and put the track back.

So, when Henry passed on without any heirs,
He willed Dartmouth the road and, as well, the repairs.
But Henry used wisdom in planning his end
For he trained Arthur Teague on whom to depend.

Arthur had talents possessed by but few,
He knew how to organize both work and the crew,
And he'd learned how to patch and make all the gadgets,
The piston and shafts, the rods and the ratchets.

But more than all this, he knew how to choose
Good men and good boys, and their best to enthuse,
With great dedication of himself to the task,
He devoted himself to his job to the last.

All's well, old traveller, the railroad's still there,
Puffing its way under Ellen's good care,
A hundred-year record covers history's pages
And God speed it safely down through the ages.

The Newcomen Society Meeting

During the summer I made a number of speeches about the Cog
Railway and its unique history. I had never done this before and felt
that I was gradually becoming more proficient. Certainly I was find-

ing it increasingly enjoyable. I wanted to do my best at the big event when the Newcomen Society would honor the railway in September.

When I finished speaking in Gilford, New Hampshire, William M. Allison, president of the Greater Laconia-Weirs Beach Chamber of Commerce, came toward me carrying a large package. I did not know what to expect and watched excitedly as he unwrapped the parcel and handed me a scroll signed by Peter S. Karagianis and himself. The scroll noted that for many years Mrs. Teague had worked side by side with her late husband, Colonel Arthur S. Teague, and after his death had carried on herself.

"We salute you humbly, but with deep admiration"; and it concluded, "as a person who has done so much, given so greatly and persevered so persistently."

I was choked with emotion but was able to voice my appreciation, saying that I was certain the mountain and the lake people would always work together for the overall good. That was one of my proudest days. How can one thank such people?

September 17 arrived, and I believe this was the second most important day of my life. My marriage was first, and now my first book containing the speech I was about to deliver, *Mount Washington Railway Company, World's First Cog Railway, Mount Washington, New Hampshire*. There it was—Library of Congress Catalog Card Number 79-93736 and copyrighted in my name—what a thrilling time for me! As I sat up on the platform I couldn't believe that all those three hundred people sitting around tables with flickering candles on each had come to hear me speak.

Following the invocation by the bishop of New Hampshire, Charles Penrose presented Governor Walter Peterson who, in turn, introduced me as follows:

My duty here tonight is to introduce a railway president and I very much doubt if this distinguished society has been host to any railway president quite like the one who is with us on this occasion.
Tonight we will all be privileged to hear from a woman whose courage, determination, capacity for hard work, and purpose of mind are familiar executive assets. But this railway president has brought charm and grace to the office which is, in my experience unique.
And the railway you will hear discussed, in its 100th anniversary year, is uncommon. It is a rare example of inventive genius, continuing human perseverance, imaginative promotion and, above all, faith.
It exemplifies faith, not only in an unusual business concept, but faith in

The "Colonel Teague" couples up under the watchful eye of Charlie Teague at the dedication ceremony in 1972.

people–people who have been, and people who continue to be, willing to spend their efforts in making something work.

The story you will hear is not simply an account of a mechanical curiosity which, by good fortune and management, has prevailed for 100 years. The story is one of remarkable biographical references, of fascinating engineering descriptions, of delightful anecdotes. It is history. But it is also a graphic picture–a picture, framed in the grandeur of old mountains and peopled by a special breed of men.

And your historian tonight is of this breed. Your speaker is not content merely to reflect on things which have made the world's first cog railway a success.

Your speaker is aware of the proud traditions which success has brought –and aware of the dedication which the people of a remarkable institution have guarded so long and expressed so well.

It is my honor and my very great pleasure to introduce to you members of Newcomen–the president of the Mount Washington Railway Company, Mrs. Ellen C. Teague.

I believe—and hope—that I rose to the occasion. I gave two introductory stories, then said, "Whatever be the undertaking we always have to leave a good deal to chance. It was assuredly so when I decided to stay with the Cog."

I put everything I had into that speech, and then it was over. I had done what I would never have dared try before, and I know it was because of the strong support I had from Charlie Penrose.

That was a memorable and rewarding experience.

Janie's Battle

September quickly disappeared into October, and it was soon time to close the railway for the season, inventory the gift shop, take stock of what would be needed in the engine shop, and put the engines and cars to bed for the winter. This took time and a lot of work. I was working in the Marshfield office one night during the first week in October when the phone rang.

"Ellen?" the voice asked. It was Margery Bargar, my nurse friend who had worked with me on the Beckurts case years before. She was now our Marshfield cashier and lived with us.

"Yes?" I had an instinctive feeling that something was wrong.

"Janie's just fallen down stairs here at the cabin. Can you come?"

I closed the Marshfield office and ran as fast as I could to the building. Here I found Janie still lying on the bottom platform of the stairway with Margery kneeling next to her. Janie was in dreadful pain, and I could see that her left leg, the one we had just healed, was twisted. Leaning down to comfort her, I realized she was in a perspiration with agony. I rushed to the telephone and dialed the Littleton Hospital. Doctor Copenhaver was on call and reassured me that he would be waiting for us. Then I called Mary Hitchcock Memorial Hospital to tell them we would come directly there from Littleton and explained the nature of our emergency.

Dr. Copenhaver met us at the door of the Littleton Clinic and immediately administered a dose of morphine to help ease Janie's pain. Then, with the help of attendants, we lifted her back into my black station wagon onto a bed fashioned of several blankets, and I started out on our fifty-seven-mile drive to Hanover. Fortunately, the state police had been notified, and a patrol car led the way so that we made the trip in record time.

As soon as we pulled up to the emergency room at Hanover, the orthopedic specialist greeted us and had Janie wheeled into the hospital and immediately examined her.

"Since this is the leg that recently healed," the doctor explained, "I don't want to place a cast on it. We've got to put it in traction, but that means anesthesia and I don't know where I'm going to find someone to administer it." Because she was a diabetic, it was difficult to persuade an anesthetist to give the anesthesia.

Providentially, Dr. Harry Bird, who was once a Cogger, heard about Janie. He was head of the anesthesia department and came to our rescue by offering to administer the anesthesia himself.

They wheeled her away, and I waited in a little room reserved for forlorn visitors like myself. I was heartbroken. It was so very sad to think that we had achieved full recovery of that leg and then puff—in a few seconds the good was all undone. Why, why, why, I kept wondering, why did this have to happen to this dear child of mine? What did the Lord have in mind? There surely must be some explanation, but it was never revealed to me.

"She's in her bed now. Would you like to see her?" a nurse asked quietly. I followed her to the four-bed room where Janie was lying, still under the influence of the anesthesia. I made certain that all her wants would be provided for and that I would be notified should any drastic change take place. Then, after taking a last look at my daughter and swallowing hard to hold back the tears, I slipped away and drove the seventy miles back to the base.

After that I went down to Hanover every night after the last train had returned to the base, stayed with Janie until midnight, and steered the black station wagon over the mountain roads back to my home. A week after we closed the railroad on Columbus Day, I moved to my Guildhall farm and started my daily commuting to Hanover from there.

Early one morning in November the phone rang. "Janie's in a coma—she's dying," the doctor said, "she's had a stroke and her right side is paralyzed completely."

"Is there any hope?" I asked, so numb I scarcely knew what I was saying. At that moment I felt like just giving up. I knew while there was life there was always hope. Suddenly I realized that my question could not be answered except by prayer.

The next few days were too blurred in my memory to record what I thought, did, or said. They insisted it was just a question of time for Janie, but I am not one to give up easily. I don't know why when the odds are so stacked against one, but Janie's life was at stake and someone had to remain optimistic, cheerful, and ready to give that extra something. My nursing experience had taught me that such an attitude often made the difference.

This latest crisis had occurred during the so-called Concord grape strike. As I sat by her bed wondering what I could do for her, I remembered that Janie had always loved grapes. Now I wonder whether it was my medical training, a woman's intuition, or perhaps divine guidance that made me feel I must get some grapes for her. Janie was receiving glucose intravenously, and I watched her just lying there, no movement in her body, lips twisted from the stroke, eyes closed—it was almost as though her very spirit had departed. Her left leg was held high off the bed in traction; she had no use of her right arm or right leg. Whenever those beautiful brown-and-hazel eyes did open, you would never suspect that she was blind. She was still such a pretty girl.

I asked Donald Moscado, the husband of the girl in the bed next to Janie, if he had any idea where I could get some wild Concord grapes.

"Leave it to me," he said, and sure enough, the following evening he brought in a basket of Concord grapes. I shall always be indebted to Donald for this act of kindness.

I immediately pealed off the skin of one of the tiny grapes and then gently squeezed the juice into Janie's mouth. She swallowed the liquid without difficulty. Emboldened, I removed the seeds and inserted the soft pulp into her mouth. She moved it about with her tongue, apparently tasting it, and then swallowed it.

Off and on for the next ten hours I repeated this, and eventually Janie ate every grape. After that I remained with her every night until eleven-thirty, giving her all the care I could. To do this I found it necessary to abandon the commuting and take a room at the nearby Occum Inn. As I signed the guest register I told the proprietor I would be there indefinitely.

Two days later when I entered Janie's room I saw that her eyes were open, and as she heard my footsteps, a faint smile played about her mouth. It was almost a miracle; the once twisted lips had straightened out and she spoke her first words: "Hello, Mum." Trembling with joy and excitement, I leaned over the bed to give her a kiss and a big hug.

Still the doctors did not give her much chance for recovery, but I started Janie on light foods, and had the intravenation removed and her insulin administered intramuscularly again. One day I went downtown and bought a large round needle and some yarn which I brought back to the hospital room. I think the doctor thought that I was the Mad Hatter, but I did not care.

I took both of Janie's hands in mine and let her feel the round knitting needle.

"It's the end of November, Janie," I told her. "Christmas is coming, so we're going to get ready for it by making a scarf."

It took all day to teach her how to put one stitch onto the needle, but once she had mastered the technique, she began to move her fingers smoothly and form the stitches on the needle. I told her we would straight-knit about ten inches and then add another color.

One morning when the doctor came in, it was evident that he couldn't believe what Janie had accomplished. Being left-handed helped, but soon she could begin to move her right arm, which greatly improved her spirits. I massaged her leg slowly each day, and finally she was able to lift it by herself. Mission accomplished!

Christmas was spent at the hospital, and all the family were there to help Janie celebrate. Presents were exchanged, but the one which meant the most to all of us was the scarf—Janie's gift for Margie. It was a beautiful sharing with love abounding, and we were able to give joy to the other patients in the room, too. After Janie ate her Christmas dinner and was fixed for the night, the rest of the family said good-bye and went to the Hanover Inn for Christmas dinner.

I had reason to be grateful, and that night I surely did thank the Almighty.

During January the orthopedic surgeon told me he did not think Janie would ever walk again. I talked with him for some time and asked when he expected to remove Janie from traction, but he told me that he could not tell until more pictures were taken. Around the middle of the month the x rays indicated that it was safe to free her leg and commence physiotherapy, but after a week of these treatments I was convinced that she would never recover in the hospital.

"The physiotherapy just won't work with Janie, I know it," I told the doctor. "Next week I'm going to sign her out and take her home to Philadelphia."

He shook his head gravely. "If you do that, you know you will have to assume all responsibility for your action."

"Yes, I know, but it's the only thing to do now."

I purchased an inflatable mattress and put it in the back of the station wagon, obtained the necessary drugs which the doctor had prescribed, and made everything ready for the trip back home.

During Janie's stay in the hospital, "Wiggles"—John Wiggand, one of our Coggers—had come down to see her several times. When he learned of my plan to drive her to Philadelphia, he said that he would follow us all the way in his VW, and if we needed help he would be there to lend assistance. I accepted his kind offer, and we made the trip without incident, stopping whenever necessary, and then going forward toward our goal.

Wiggles carried Janie upstairs, and I could see the happy expression on her face when he put her down on her own bed. Once home Janie brightened up and wanted to sit in a chair. Several days later I got her up, and soon she was walking to the bathroom by herself, feeling her way along the wall.

She was great; she had won her battle!

My Trying Time

With Janie safely returned home I was able to devote some time to the railroad again. Since Lionel had informed me that he would not return in 1970 as manager, I had to select someone else.

The new man did a good job his first year, although he was not the ideal man, having a very cold personality. He did tell me when I hired him that he always stopped work at five to have his before-dinner drink, but that did not concern me. He was evidently interested in his career, for he asked if he could buy stock in the company. I had to tell him that was impossible, as all the stock was to remain in the Teague family.

During the 1971 season I noticed that his attitude had changed. I watched our employees carefully and could see the changes which had taken place in their attitudes. He began playing up to the employees and hosted frequent beer parties at the cabin where he and his wife lived. Soon two of our employees who had always been very friendly to us hardly spoke to me or other members of the family. Then another employee began to treat the manager with marked deference, and I began to wonder what he was telling them.

One day I found out. He had been telling the employees that I used the Cog money to take winter trips, and they believed every word he told them. Somehow he seemed to inspire confidence, especially

The newest engine, "Colonel Teague," and the oldest coach, No. 1, at Base Station in 1978.

when he was lying. Walter, one of my most loyal friends and who had been with us for years, told me that the manager would ask him why he liked me.

All of this upset me very much and made my work and Janie's most unpleasant. More about this man later.

Honors and Problems for the Cog

In August 1971 the New Hampshire State Historical Commission wrote to see if its members could hold their meeting here at the base and then ride the train to the summit. I invited them to my home for lunch after their meeting and arranged for them to go up the mountain. It was a beautiful day, and everything went well. I should like to share their letter of thanks, which read:

Dear Mrs. Teague:
In addition to our personal thanks, the Historical Commission would like to
express to you an official thank you for the most delightful excursion and
luncheon which you so kindly provided for our August meeting.
Climbing Mount Washington via your Cog Railway afforded the Commis-
sion a most unique opportunity to observe at first hand one of our primary
historical attractions here in New Hampshire. We are all proud to belong to
the organization which so many years earlier recognized this facility as
being most worthy of an historical marker.

Two months later Joe Dodge, the famous hutmaster at the AMC
Pinkham Notch Hut, wrote inviting Margie and me to have dinner
with him and his wife, Teen, before the annual meeting of the Conway Historical Society, at which I was to speak along with Henry
Waldo. Meetings of this sort gave me a splendid opportunity to tell
others about the Cog Railway and what we were trying to do for the
state. At the same time, a speaking engagement of this kind often was
the means of stirring up renewed interest in an organization, because
members who rarely attended meetings came out to learn more about
the famous railroad.

Janie and I returned to the base early in June 1972. Trouble was
brewing, and this time it was a subject called "air pollution" and a
man by the name of Forrest Bumford. I have learned over the years
that when one is in business there are always problems to solve. The
important thing is to decide how to solve them, and then get the job
done.

We had been informed that our steam locomotives were polluting
the mountains in violation of the air pollution law, and we had been
served with a formal order by the New Hampshire Air Pollution
Commission to stop operating our locomotives. I felt that we had been
unjustly treated and that this made no sense whatever. It soon became
evident from articles and letters in various newspapers that others
agreed with me.

My lawyer advised me to apply for a variance, but I was not
convinced as I would have to do this every two years, and the winds of
political change could disqualify us at the whim of some politician.
Instead, I felt that we must either win or lose by doing battle now. I
took a chance and contacted Senator Laurier Lamontagne to request
his help. He and Mrs. Green, chairman of the Air Pollution Commission, spearheaded the necessary legislative action to exclude steam

locomotives from the provisions of the air pollution act, thus solving the problem permanently.

The following letter was received by Forrest Bumford, administrative director of the Air Pollution Commission:

Dear Sir:

In regard to your recent order to the Mount Washington Cog Railway to stop operation of their steam locomotives I wish to go on record as very much opposed to this action by your Commission.

The Cog Railway steam locomotives were designed to burn soft coal and no other fuel would be efficient, economical or practical. Also your commission should realize that much of the attraction of the Cog Railway is the fact that steam engines are used and that they do put out smoke, steam and noise. Taking the unique steam locomotives off the Cog Railway would make as much sense as shutting off the water over Niagara Falls because it causes too much mist in the air. The Cog Railway and its steam engines have become a permanent part of the White Mountain scene and must remain so.

The fine people who own and operate this railway are performing a great service in perpetuating this enterprise for this and future generations. They certainly do not deserve to be harassed for their efforts.

I would respectfully suggest that the efforts of your commission would be better directed towards the elimination of the noxious exhaust fumes and noise put out by the hundreds of huge diesel trucks that roar over every highway in the State day and night. Surely that presents a more serious problem than a little coal smoke which is quickly dissipated over rocky wilderness by the winds of Mount Washington.

I am very proud of the letter I received from Representative Myrtle B. Rogers, which read:

Thank you, for your continued search for low sulphur coal. I for one am glad you have had some success.

As a member of the House Environment and Agriculture Committee, I voted for exempting the Cog Railway from the Air Pollution Law, because my family has always considered the railway a landmark in our fair state.

It is heartening to find someone like Representative Rogers willing to go the second mile. So often in life when we lend a helping hand, that hand becomes a permanent crutch.

I tried to work out my problems, and they usually turned out for the best if I didn't hurry my solutions. Once the pollution matter was settled, we had to get ready for the inaugural run of the Col. Arthur S. Teague locomotive.

I invited numerous people to come and see us cut the ribbons for her first trip. Governor Wesley Powell was on hand, and Senator Lamontagne supported the "takeoff." My son Charles had been flown up from Stony Brook School on Long Island by my friend, Joe O'Brien of Twin Mountain, so that he could be the brakeman on the passenger coach, which was to be pushed up the track by the locomotive named for his father. It was a most successful day and a fine tribute to my husband.

The Cog Manager Cooks His Own Goose

The year 1972 slipped away, and soon I was busy preparing for our 1973 season. Janie and I began to line up Marshfield House employees early in January because we hoped to have a good group of Coggers. It made a difference to the tourists if they were treated well, and we wanted them to comment favorably on the attitudes and work performance of all the men and women who worked at the Cog Railway.

Fanny said that she would manage the kitchen again. She was a good worker and the employees got along well with her, which explained why so many of them returned year after year. We were lucky there. Most of our employees were college students; a few had completed their education. Usually we had an older group of workers during the fall season, since the younger ones had returned to school.

When Janie, Fanny, and I arrived at the base early in June, we found it difficult to understand why the Railway employees seemed so cold in their attitude toward us.

Late that June when Janie and I returned one evening from the Weathervane Theater in Whitefield I saw a note pinned to my door saying that there was a meeting at the boardinghouse. I drove there immediately and found many of the Railway employees sitting about full of talk, complaints, and beer. Their abusive talk was sickening, and since they would not listen to me, I left.

Next I heard that a strike was planned for the Fourth of July. What had happened now?

To prevent the strike from working, I secretly contacted several of our former loyal employees—engineers, firemen, and brakemen —enough for three crews to be on hand. I was right. On July 4 none of the manager's crews came to work, but I had two crews with a reserve on hand. Dr. Bob Campbell took over one of the locomotives as engineer; Joe McQuaid, later editor of *The Union Leader*, took over the second engine; and the spare remained at the base.

The railway opened for business, but no one was permitted to answer the phone at the ticket office. One of the strikers put a plug in the switch at the base. Meanwhile another had called the Public Utility Commission saying that we were operating against rules. I learned of this through a friend at Troop F. Then I called my lawyer, Jack Middleton.

The manager asked for a contract and demanded that Mrs. Teague and Janie leave or he would go. Since the season was already under way, I had no alternative, because without a manager the Public Utility Commission would have closed the Cog. Janie and I decided to go to Kennebunkport, Maine, but Fanny had to stay, since she was in charge of the kitchen. As soon as I could get her things together, Janie and I left for Maine.

Janie had been working continually at the cash register in Marshfield even though blind. She had put up a small sign which read, "I Am Blind," and was able to make change easily, although she sometimes had to ask one of the girls to help with the bills. The job had kept her happy and busy, it being the best thing for her diabetes to keep active. When we left, Janie became very depressed and grew more and more so as the weeks went by. Finally she became very ill at Kennebunkport, so I decided to return to my house at the base and take her to the doctor in Lancaster, New Hampshire.

When I returned, Fanny, who had been living in my home, came to see us right away. After that, Janie and I did not go to the base again for the rest of the season. Later my loyal bookkeeper, Ken Randall, came down to see me and reported conditions.

In the midst of all this unhappiness we experienced the worst tragedy of all. Janie Teague died early in the morning of October 14. I felt as though a large part of me had gone with her. Had Fanny not been there to sustain me, I doubt that I could have gotten through the next few days. The first thing I did after the undertaker had taken her body away was to go to the base and put the flag at half-mast. Following the funeral at Saint Paul's Church in Lancaster, Janie was buried beside her sister, Lucy.

Two friends who gave me extra help and comfort through this period were Lila and Earl Cone. They took Janie and me out many evenings when I needed the change but could not have managed alone, and more important, they shared my problems with great sympathy and understanding.

My next manager was Eddie Clark of Clark's Trading Post in Lincoln, New Hampshire. Eddie had an engineering degree from the marines and had served in World War II. He had his good and bad points, as we all have, but he came to my rescue after the previous manager was dismissed.

A New Year, a New Start

It was evident that 1974 would be the year to get a number of things straightened out at the railway. Eddie Clark was kind to me. The biggest job was to restore the distorted feelings of our employees. We got going slowly and it took time to break in the new employees, but it was worth the effort.

Just before I had left for the mountains Fanny was married on May 24 to Robert Blaggie of Twin Mountain, New Hampshire. The wedding was held at Saint-Martin-in-the-Fields, and her reception was at the Philadelphia Cricket Club. Fanny looked beautiful and her wedding could not have been nicer. It was a festive affair with loads of her friends present, and it was gratifying to see many of Fanny's former school pupils sitting in the church.

That summer I found it very hard to work at the base without Janie and Fanny, whom I missed very much. Fortunately, Charles was with me now, living in his own home at the base.

One day during the summer Alexander Hamilton, who had given the invocation at our centennial celebration, dropped in at the base to see me. He had been good to Janie and had been up several times this summer, but I had scarcely noticed him. What with Janie's illness and other problems at the railway, I did not have a single moment to think about other things or people.

Alex somehow awoke me to my true self and inspired new feelings which were difficult to describe. I had been dead within ever since Art died, and now I had a new excited feeling after all these years. Gradually I became alive and happy inside. I wanted to reach out to others and be loved.

Alex was never soft-spoken but somewhat abrupt and on the rough side. It took me several years to understand him, and then I found that underneath his abruptness he was unsure of himself. It was a cover-up. Knowing this, I wanted to help him. Our meetings were quite casual. We were such opposites that at first it was difficult for us to understand each other. Alex was an unusual person—not only an ordained Episcopal priest, but a trolley and railroad buff as well, having been one of the prime movers in establishing and developing the Kennebunkport Trolley Museum in Maine.

Eddie Clark and I struggled through that season, and we were both mighty glad when Columbus Day came. He had much to learn about opening and closing the railway.

The following year, 1975, went better. Business improved, and I felt more like my old self. I saw Alex off and on, and although I did not pay that much attention to him, I had to admit to myself that I felt differently when he was with me.

I was a member of the Royal Academy of Science, being made a member by Sir James Taylor of London, and had an invitation to participate in the academy's celebration to be held in November. A number of members of the Newcomen Society who also belonged to the Royal Society planned to attend the big event in London. I casually asked Alex if he would be interested in going with us, and he said yes. We flew to London, were entertained royally, presented to Prince Philip, and visited the house where Benjamin Franklin stayed while in London. Many of these special events were arranged just for the "Benjamin Franklin Fellows" of the United States, to which I also belonged. Our group attended a session of Parliament, followed by a special buffet luncheon in the Parliament building overlooking the Thames, after which we were entertained by the American ambassador.

Alex and I then flew to Ireland and lunched with Cornelius Cremin and his wife, who lived on the Ring of Kerry. "Con" had recently retired as Ireland's representative to the United Nations where he served as chairman of the committee concerned with the laws of the sea.

It was all very exciting, and especially so because I felt it was a new life for me and I felt alive being with Alex.

The Cog Becomes an Engineering Landmark

In 1976 I had to prepare for another celebration at the Cog Railway on June 26. We were to be cited as an engineering landmark.

The night before the dedication the American Society of Mechanical Engineers and the American Society of Civil Engineers gave a dinner at the New England Inn in Intervale. It was a lot of fun, and Eddie Clark delivered an outstanding speech about the Cog Railway. The following day I set up a podium and 200 chairs in the lobby of Marshfield House. I believe we had around 250 engineers crowded into the room. After we had listened to several speakers, the Cog Railway was presented with a plaque by both societies, acting jointly for the first time. The railway was recognized by this citation as a National Historic Engineering landmark, and the bronze plaque was subsequently affixed to the boulder where Art's plaque was dedicated in his memory by the Coggers.

A Typical Day

So many people, on learning that I was president of the railway, appeared astounded and asked what I did, as though this was either an impossible task or so out of the ordinary that a woman could never fill the post. For the benefit of those readers who are curious too, I shall tell briefly what happens on a typical day during the railway season, assuming for the moment that I am still running the Cog —which I'm not. At this time my son, Charles Teague, has been president for the past three years.

I awake early, around five-thirty, perhaps because of my nurse's training when it was routine to arise with the birds. A hot bath not only refreshes me but seems to give me the necessary energy for the day ahead. After dressing according to weather requirements, I literally grab my fruit juice and toast which I eat rapidly, and then pick up the black box with the tickets and cash which I take with me to the hikers' parking lot.

I should mention here that many hikers have been coming to the west slope of Mount Washington, and we found it necessary to provide a parking lot just for their use. Previously they parked in the lots by Marshfield Station, and our train passengers had difficulty parking their cars. Six o'clock in the morning is a lovely time of day when I feel free and relaxed and enjoy meeting the arriving hikers.

"Which trail are you taking today?" I would ask one. "The Jewel or Ammonoosuc?" "How many nights will you be up there?" "The Weather Observatory promises a fine day for you," or vice versa. I am always prepared to give the latest weather information, which I receive from the summit before leaving my house.

The regular parking attendant relieves me at eight-thirty, enabling me to drive to Marshfield House to check the ticket office and see who is on duty, review the train crew schedule, and make certain that all is well. As the employees report in I greet them and am rewarded with a cheerful "Good morning, Mrs. Teague." Meanwhile, the mail truck has arrived from Littleton, and now I must open up the post office.

In 1967 after Art died, I put in my bid to become mail clerk for the railway so that the Mount Washington Rural Branch Post Office could be retained. When the mail arrives I pick up the bags, take them to my Marshfield office to sort and then distribute the letters to our employees' mailbox in the kitchen. The bag containing mail for the summit I give to the brakeman of the first scheduled train, and it is his responsibility to deliver it to an authorized person up there.

After this I answer all of the correspondence which has come in that morning and check with the bookkeeper to make certain that the various departments are making proper financial reports.

Around a quarter of eleven I usually go to the kitchen in order to check on the food orders, as well as the day's menu for the employees, the cafeteria, and the lunch counter. Then back to the office for telephone calls and consultations with employees, followed by lunch.

Next I make my afternoon round through the lobby, check for trash and litter, make certain the tables are clean, and take a quick walk through the gift shop. My inspection trip is constantly interrupted by greetings and questions from friends and strangers, all in all a very happy experience for me.

On tour days I try to make it a point of getting aboard each arriving bus and personally welcoming the visitors to the railway. This enables me to give them some information about their trip which will

WALTER MITCHELL joined us in 1963, and each spring came from his winter teaching job to his hobby of railroading. He especially enjoyed his steam train ride each morning and evening as he went to and from the summit. There he served as the postal clerk. According to Leon Anderson, "Mount Washington's prestige has earned it the distinction of being an official part of the United States Postal Service."

make it more enjoyable. Most tours make advance arrangements to have the people eat in the cafeteria, and if they plan to take the two o'clock train they generally eat around one. This means that I will be on hand there to help the girls wherever needed to get the large crowd through in time for the scheduled departure.

About two-thirty I become the postal clerk again and collect the postcards and letters from the mailbox and cancel them. At the same time I complete any post office reports which must be sent to Twin Mountain and Littleton post offices. Sometimes there can be a lot of bookkeeping, involving stamp sales, registered and certified letters, and other special transactions. By three o'clock the summit mail has come down to the base and I have the mail bags ready for the truck when it pulls in around four. All the mail goes to Littleton, then is placed on trucks destined for White River Junction, Vermont, where it is processed.

About four-thirty I try to return to my home and rest for a half hour, but I keep the plant phone by my side. Faith Bencosky, my loyal secretary and dispatcher, who has been with me for seven years, knows that if she needs me she is not to hesitate to call.

Supper is served to the employees from four-thirty to seven and I remain on hand in case I am needed. I always wait until the last train has come down the mountain and discharged its passengers. Before returning home I check to make certain Marshfield House has been closed properly, toilets are locked, and that the various financial statements for the day are in order. Alex Hamilton helps me with these chores. He also remains in the ticket office until the end of the day as night dispatcher and to answer visitors' questions. With the office locked up, the engines put to bed, and the employees fed, I am ready to relax.

Some days are long, and some fly by and are gone before I know it. Frequently I make it a point to ride the trains just to make sure that everything is going as it should. Joe O'Brien frequently flies me over the track and trains in his Piper plane so that I can inspect from above. A few days are frustrating, but most of them are satisfying, especially when I receive letters of appreciation. Complaints are at a minimum. Regardless of what happens my faith sustains me, and I share my prayers each evening with Father Alex Hamilton. God comforts me in my troubles and tribulations and rewards me richly with many blessings.

Ever since my heart attack following Art's death, I have had to take

EMPLOYEES' TIMETABLE

Daily 6/25 through 9/5/1977 (Trains 4401–4420) — **Daily 9/6 through 10/10/1977** (Trains 4451–4454)

Train (ascending)

Stations	Elevation			4401	4403	4405	4407	4409	4411	4413	4415	4417	4419	4451	4453
Base (Shop)	2550	w	LV	0800	0900	1000	1100	1200	0100	0200	0300	0400	0500	1000	0200
Bunker		c	LV												
Marshfield	2700	w	AR	0818	0918	1018	1118	1218	0118	0218	0318	0418	0518	1018	0218
Marshfield			LV												
Waumbeck	3700	w	AR	0823	0923	1029	1129	1229	0129	0229	0329	0429	0529	1023	0223
Waumbeck			LV												
Half Way	4300		AR	0836	0936	1041	1141	1241	0141	0241	0341	0441	0541	1036	0236
Half Way			LV												
Skyline	5650	c	AR	0857	0957	1100	1200	0100	0200	0300	0400	0500	0600	1057	0257
Skyline			LV	0858	0959	1101	1201	0101	0201	0301	0401	0501	0601	1058	0258
Gulf	5800	w	AR	0903	1003	1106	1206	0106	0206	0306	0406	0506	0606	1103	0303
Gulf			LV												
Summit	6265	w	AR	0910	1010	1115	1215	0115	0215	0315	0415	0515	0615	1111	0311

Train (descending) — Bent

Stations	Elevation		4402	4404	4406	4408	4410	4412	4414	4416	4418	4420	4452	4454
Summit	1220	LV	0940	1040	1140	1240	0140	0240	0340	0440	0540	0640	1140	0340
Gulf	1010	AR	0950	1050	1150	1250	0150	0250	0350	0450	0550	0650	1150	0350
Gulf		LV												
Skyline	900	AR	0957	1057	1157	1257	0157	0257	0357	0457	0557	0657	1157	0357
Skyline		LV												
Half Way	590	AR	1004	1105	1205	0105	0205	0305	0405	0505	0605	0705	1205	0405
Half Way		LV												
Waumbeck	375	AR	1018	1118	1218	0118	0218	0318	0418	0518	0618	0718	1210	0410
Waumbeck		LV												
Marshfield	5	AR	1026	1126	1226	0126	0226	0326	0426	0526	0626	0726	1219	0419
Marshfield		LV	1027	1127	1227	0127	0227	0327	0427	0527	0627	0727	1220	0420
Bunker		AR												
Base (Shop)		AR	1040	1140	1240	0140	0240	0340	0440	0540	0640	0740	1233	0433

Legend: w—water stop; c—coaling stop; bent—track marker

medication daily and try to regulate my activities. Dr. Andrew Ross of Littleton has been my left hand in guiding me medically with my cardiology problems, administering my medication, reassuring me that I can continue to lead a normal life, and pulling me through some dangerous attacks.

"Old Peppersass" Gets Unusual Recognition

July 8, 1978, was a historic day because dual ceremonies were held on Mount Washington, one at the summit, the other at the base. On the summit we had the ground breaking for the new $3 million summit building which would be named the Sherman Adams Building. Governor Thomson was on hand and invited me to join the special group which included former Governor Adams with his sporty outfit and his well-known "chapeau," as well as former Governors Hugh Gregg and Lane Dwinell.

Following the ceremony everyone took a special train for the second event to be held before *Old Peppersass*. Here the notables were joined by Charles Teague, president and manager of the railway; Leon Anderson, legislative historian who had written and published a special booklet for the occasion; and Costas Tentas, chairman of the New Hampshire Liquor Commission. A specially designed *Peppersass* decanter was presented to Governor Thomson, after which the decanters were placed on sale inside Marshfield House. It was a day to be remembered! Betty and Lane Dwinell were always with us on important occasions, and both of them gave me big hugs, after which Sherm, looking so perky with his bow tie, also gave me a bigger bear hug. I felt I had received more attention than *Old Peppersass* herself! Frances Ann Johnson Hancock wrote a poem about this event which is reprinted below.

OLD PEPPERSASS (1869-1969)

1.

Sylvester Marsh of Campton Town
Had an inventive streak.
He planned a railway to ascend
New Hampshire's highest peak.
He claimed an engine could be built
To push a loaded train
Right up atop Mount Washington
And ease it down again.

I Conquered My Mountain

Chorus

That engine was Old Peppersass,
Unrivaled in her prime.
And now she's back beside the track
She was the first to climb.

2.

Marsh had to get a charter first,
So to the State applied.
But all the Legislators laughed
And laughed until they cried.
They even called him "Crazy Marsh,"
As crazy as a loon.
Perhaps he'd like a track to take
His engine to the moon!

3.

He got the charter, then perceived
He still must build alone.
Folks wouldn't risk their money, so—
He had to risk his own.
He laid the track up Cold Spring Hill,
A slope of Washington,
Then hauled by ox team all the parts
That make an engine run.

4.

The engine boiler stood up straight
To make the steepest grade,
Like an old bottle, long of neck,
For pepper sauces made.
So she was known as Peppersass
Through twelve exciting years
Of pushing up and backing down
By means of cogs and gears.

5.

Then she was loaned to several Fairs
Far from Mount Washington.
And in a distant museum
Met near oblivion,
Until, years later, she was found
And brought back home to stay.
New Hampshire welcomed her return
And held a Gala Day.

6.

And now, upon a tilted track
The engine stands at rest.
She's facing up, as in past years,
Toward the Mountain's crest.
And while crowds travel up and down
And newer engines pass,
The glory of her youth still lives
In grand Old Peppersass!

Of Managers and Coal Mines

Ed Clark had left us the fall of 1976. One most helpful thing Ed accomplished was to build us the "speeder." This little-track skimobile contraption saved the railway employees time when we had breakdowns because it enabled the men to take the tools up quickly, instead of sending up a much slower steam locomotive.

After Ed left I began to look for another manager, as Charles was not ready for the job. Alex and I gave it a lot of thought, and he suggested a friend of his, George Burdick, who was associated with the Kennebunk Trolley Museum in Maine. We thereupon approached him and submitted his name to my lawyer and to the Public Utility Commission. Both approved of our choice.

George was a good engineer and did well working with electrical equipment. He made a great improvement in our power system, installing automatic controls on the current so that we no longer had to run to the engine shop whenever the lights became too hot and bright. He was a fine engineer.

Charlie Teague worked with us summers while attending technology college, and he, George, and I got along together very well. What one couldn't do, the other tried. I saw many improvements around the engine shop, the grounds, and Marshfield House. Charles became manager in 1979, and George remained as chief engineer. As Charlie put it, he "worked his butt off."

Early in 1980, after he had completed all of his orders for the summer, Charles called me in Philadelphia and asked if I would care to go with him to West Virginia where he planned to visit some of the mines to buy coal. What a spree we had! I enjoyed every moment of it, for I had never been in that section of the country, let alone down in a coal mine.

Approaching the Summit, with the new Sherman Adams Summit Building in the background.

After visiting the Bethlehem, Grafton, and La Rosa mining companies in Clarksburg, West Virginia, we drove to Jane Lew to talk with a coal expert, as Charles had not found exactly what he wanted for his bituminous coal supply. Next we headed to Nettie and the Pittston Corporation where we were invited to take a tour of the mine.

After a sandwich and a soft drink, I donned a pair of overalls, put my emergency kit onto my belt, clapped a helmet on my head, and signed a paper absolving the mine from all responsibility should there be an accident. Charles laughed heartily when he saw his mother in this outfit. Sam Sapp, the district engineer, led us to an electric jeep, and off we went into the mine, down, down, down, several miles under the riverbed. It was a thrilling experience, and as a souvenir the engineer brought back a two-foot piece of coal for me to take home. From there we went to Kentucky and then back to Philadelphia to prepare for the 1980 season.

Throughout the summer, the state was in a dither getting ready to open and dedicate the new Sherman Adams Building on the Summit. It was to be Friday, September 5, 1980.

The day arrived, and there couldn't have been worse weather. It was rainy, foggy, and really nasty with gusts of high winds, a storm indeed. We were overrun with the invited guests who wanted to ride the railway to the crown of Mount Washington, to see the new building, and hear Sherman Adams speak at the dedication.

It was a very special affair; everyone we knew was there. Governor Adams looked so proud as he read his speech complimenting all those who had helped complete his dream of this new building, which would go down in state park history. He ended his talk this way:

For my association with this project I shall always owe a debt of gratitude to Walter Peterson and to Mel Thomson, for this has been for me a great and rare opportunity to become a part of the annals of history which hold for all time the story of the pride and the care which the people of this state will always feel for their greatest mountain.

That was Sherm and he spoke beautifully. Then a delicious buffet supper was served by the state, and when the train left at seven-fifteen to come down the mountain, the rain was pouring harder than before and the winds were howling fiercely. The mountain was giving us its cruelest blasts as we loaded the guests back onto the Cog Railway trains.

I sat with Governor Lane Dwinell all the way to the base. He and Betty are among my best friends. I tried to talk with so many, but one can't reach them all, although I did have a good talk with Congressman James Cleveland.

Tell me what the people would do without those trains on a day and night like that? Not many dared go down the carriage road because of the weather, but the old Cog proved its worth once again.

Difficulties with the Public Utility Commission

My last year with the railway was not to be the easiest. As I mentioned previously, we operate subject to the authorization of the New Hampshire Public Utility Commission. There are times when it is difficult to understand the mental gyrations of such a body, and in 1981 I had my most difficult experience with this bureaucratic commission.

We prepared as usual to open Memorial Day weekend, which we did, had our help all on hand, food purchased, trains in running order, and the commission's approval to operate, when lo—without warning the following weekend—the commission shut down the railway. It refused to permit us to operate to the halfway point, as we had always done when trackwork had to be done on the upper part of the railway. An inspector was not satisfied with the condition of the ties on the stretch of track between Lizzie Bourne's marker and the summit, and accordingly it was decided to issue an order to halt all operations until the replacement of those ties was completed.

Looking back on the incident, I recall that I did not want to do anything which might antagonize the commission and thus have delayed its approval to operate. I was disappointed, however, as trackwork was progressing as planned. I had always cooperated with the commission in every possible way, and to be subjected to a total close down seemed more than unfortunate. We started the season with a discouraging deficit, but I harbor no hard feelings.

Once the season got under way business picked up. By Columbus Day, when we closed, more than fifty thousand passengers had made the trip to the summit. Again the engines and coaches have been put to bed, the pipes blown out, the water turned off, the various buildings boarded and closed for the winter, and the shutters drawn. Since the railway is an operating museum, it is guarded during the winter months by the caretaker, Crawford Hassen, who has been *en garde* for many years.

This 1981 closing was different for me, though. I had decided to sell the Railway but only when I had found the person who would continue faithfully to preserve and operate Sylvester Marsh's unique enterprise as long as people want to ride to Mt. Washington's summit. Then I will enter that mythical state of "retirement."

Epilogue

ELLEN OPENED *the front door of Marshfield House, then turned to take a last look at the lobby. This room had been an important part of her life for more than three decades, and it was not easy to leave tonight. Parting from the railway was like listening as her daughters repeated their wedding vows. Marriage and death separated her from her girls, but they would always be bound together by love. Why wouldn't it be the same with the railway? She would no longer be actively involved, but she could offer the new owner her services as a consultant, perhaps sit on the board of directors, and thus not lose touch. Just as she had prayed that Margie, Fanny, and Anne would be wise in selecting their partners, she hoped that her choice of a new owner for the Cog would be the right one. It should be someone who understood the importance of tourism, politics, and good relations with employees and neighbors, but most of all someone who loved the railway and the mountains.*

As she snapped off the lights, pulled the door shut and locked it, that nagging doubt returned. Would she be happy without the excitement, the glamour, and the daily challenges which even a tiny railway could bring to its owner? Should she willingly settle for another kind of life which would not include the Cog?

She walked slowly toward her car and paused, thinking of all that had happened here in this forest clearing since Sylvester Marsh had built the railway more than 112 years ago. She had been a part of this heritage handed down by Marsh, and she had done her job as best she could, but wasn't it time now for younger blood and new ideas to filter into this historic railway? Swinging about, she faced Mount Washington, now barely visible in the dusk, and she knew what her decision must be.

Base Station and "Old Peppersass" in the solitude of winter.

One day, looking up at the summit when she was thinking about Art and their family, it occurred to Ellen that everyone has a mountain to conquer. For some it is a low hill, for others a Mount Washington. Poor Lucy's was low, for she had scarcely started life, and dear Janie's was not much higher, but both girls had courageously climbed as high as their brief life spans permitted. Art had conquered his too, but in struggling toward that last rock on the summit he lost his grip. Now Anne in Deerfield Street, New Jersey, Fanny in Bedford, New Hampshire, and Margie in Montgomery County, Pennsylvania, were on their way up their mountains, and son Charlie too was in full gear as he looked forward to returning to college and preparing for a lifetime career "Elsewhere"!

"I conquered my mountain," Ellen said aloud, her voice carrying both conviction and pride, for it summed up exactly how she felt. This evening, this very moment, she was at the top. Her four loves had helped her along the way—first nursing, then marriage, followed by the children, and finally her assumption of responsibility for running the railway.

Soon she too would start down the other side into the valley known as retirement—an easier trip, but it could be every bit as exciting and full of adventure. There was still so much to be done—a book to be written about her life and loves, a new home to be built in Whitefield, children and grandchildren to be visited and loved, and always new ways to be of help to friends and strangers wherever she might be.

The stars and the moon were appearing overhead and a light breeze brought with it the faint scent of spruce. As she started toward her car, her walk was brisk, her head was high, and she felt a new sense of purpose. She had conquered her mountain, and now a new life lay before her.

Illustrations and Credits

Although the great majority of the illustrative material appearing in *I Conquered My Mountain* came from the files of the author, many other sources were explored and the publisher is deeply grateful to all who so generously offered their help. In the following, photographs are listed in the order in which they appear in the volume, and the identifying caption of each is followed by the name of the photographer, where known. The line drawings appearing at the beginning of each chapter are from *The Mount Washington Railway Company*, by Ellen C. Teague, published in 1969 by the Newcomen Society in North America.

Jacket photo of author by Elvira Murdoch, Mount Washington / Fabyan. Jacket photo of train from the author's files, photographer unknown. Endleaf photo of trains, courtesy of White Mountain News Bureau, photographer unknown.

Marshfield Base under construction, 1870 / page 4.

At the Summit, early 1870s / page 6.

"Old Peppersass" / courtesy Littleton *Courier* / page 8.

Coach No. 2 at the Summit / Dick Smith, North Conway / page 10.

Marker at Fabyan Station / Harold Orne, Melrose, Mass., / page 14.

The author at seven / page 20.

The author in nursing school / page 30.

Approaching the Summit / page 36.

Looking toward Marshfield Station / Douglas B. Grundy,
    Franconia / page 38.

Arthur S. Teague / page 47.

Rotogravure photo of "Socialite Ellen Crawford" / page 53.

Waumbek engine and Chumley coach / F. F. Zimmerman, Media,
    Pa. / page 56.

The "family" before Art went overseas. / page 58.

Mt. Washington from the Base / Elvira Murdock / page 60.

Henry Nelson Teague at the Flamingo Hotel / page 66.

B&M coach passengers at Fabyan, 1906 / Peter Eddy, Fabyan House /
    page 68.

Train crew in the early 1920s / Blackington Service, Boston, Mass. /
    page 70.
